SPORTSMAN
ENVIRONMENTALIST

Tom Mullikin

Vox Populi Publishers, LLC
100 North Tryon Street, Suite 4700
Charlotte, NC 28202-4003

10 9 8 7 6 5 4 3 2 1

ISBN   978-0-9790178-7-2

Copyright © 2009 by Vox Populi Publishers, LLC

All rights reserved. No part of this publication may be reproduced, stored in a retrieval system, or transmitted in any form or by any means, electronic, mechanical, photocopy, recording, or otherwise, without the prior written permission of the publisher.

Printed in the United States of America.

Contents

Acknowledgements	v
America's Sporting Heritage	3
Conservation Takes Root in American Soil	13
The Growth of Modern Conservation	35
What You Should Know about Climate Change	69
Creating Sound Social Policy	93
How to Reduce Your Environmental Footprint	109

ACKNOWLEDGMENTS

For generations my family has enjoyed the beautiful outdoors. My father, a World War II veteran and decorated hero, first taught me to appreciate our environment, enjoy safe hunting and fair chase. My grandfather, a World War I veteran, taught me to enjoy a day on the open water taking only those fish that were going to be eaten and practicing catch and release – long before it became a popular practice among anglers. I first want to acknowledge both of these men for my appreciation of a sustainable and beautiful environment.

As for the thoughts contained within this book, I would mostly like to thank my team at Moore & Van Allen, starting with my good friend and colleague Todd Muldrew. Todd (a.k.a. Wiz) has been the greatest researcher, writer and manager that I could ever have hoped to have. I would also like to thank John Hofland, Joel Groves, Jackie Parker and Marie Hochstein, who have given invaluable support in helping bring this project to a conclusion. These men and women work with my most talented and capable senior partners, Nancy Smith and John Saydlowski, who take on more and more projects, yet always ensure a timely and high quality work product.

Finally, I would like to thank my close friends with whom I have experienced some of the most enjoyable hunting and fishing trips around the world: Chris Culler, with whom I have grown up hunting and fishing in the Carolinas, Alaska and Texas; Randy Sexton, who has made some of the best gator hunts in the bayou of Louisiana:

Fred Bezentenhuit, with whom I have hunted plains game and the Big Five in Africa; Ross Gerko, with whom I have shark hunted in many waters around the world; and my constant hunting and traveling companion, Peter "Rock" Allen.

Finally, it is my greatest hope that this book will inspire hunters and anglers around the world to continue enjoying the outdoors and to serve as working ambassadors for a clean and healthy environment both for our generation, and for many more generations to come.

SPORTSMAN
ENVIRONMENTALIST

Tom Mullikin

AMERICA'S SPORTING HERITAGE

"We have fallen heirs to the most glorious heritage a people ever received, and each one must do his part if we wish to show that the nation is worthy of its good fortune."
—Theodore Roosevelt

It is believed that North America used to be home to over 60 million buffalo—more than the entire human population of the Great Plains today.[1] By 1893, only 300 buffalo resided there.[2] The shocking disappearance of the great herds inspired the formation of the American Bison Society in 1905, with sitting United States President Theodore Roosevelt as its honorary president.

Roosevelt had numerous encounters with the buffalo and the men who hunted them during his time as a rancher in the Midwest. His own pleasure in hunting buffalo caused him to lament the loss of the beasts in his book, *Hunting Trips of a Ranchman*. Roosevelt pointedly wrote that "from a purely selfish standpoint many, including myself, would rather see [the buffalo] continue to exist as the chief feature in the unchanged life of the Western wilderness."[3] He regales readers with one of his less-than-successful encounters with a group of buffalo:

> As we cantered toward them they faced us for a second and then turned round and made off, while with spurs and quirts we made the ponies put on a burst that enabled

us to close in with the wounded one just about the time that the lessening twilight had almost vanished; while the rim of the full moon rose above the horizon. The pony I was on could barely hold its own, after getting up within sixty or seventy yards of the wounded bull; my companion, better mounted, forged ahead, a little to one side. The bull saw him coming and swerved from his course, and by cutting across I was able to get nearly up to him. The ground over which we were running was fearful, being broken into holes and ditches, separated by hillocks; in the dull light, and at the speed we were going, no attempt could be made to guide the horses, and the latter, fagged out by their exertions, floundered and pitched forward at every stride, hardly keeping their legs. When up within twenty feet I fired my rifle, but the darkness, and especially the violent, labored motion of my pony, made me miss; I tried to get in closer, when suddenly up went the bull's tail, and wheeling, he charged me with lowered horns. My pony, frightened into momentary activity, spun round and tossed up his head; I was holding the rifle in both hands, and the pony's head, striking it, knocked it violently against my forehead, cutting quite a gash, from which, heated as I was, the blood poured into my eyes. Meanwhile the

> buffalo, passing me, charged my companion, and followed him as he made off, and, as the ground was very bad, for some little distance his lowered head was unpleasantly near the tired pony's tail. I tried to run in on him again, but my pony stopped short, deadbeat; and by no spurring could I force him out of a slow trot. My companion jumped off and took a couple of shots at the buffalo, which missed in the dim moonlight; and to our unutterable chagrin the wounded bull labored off and vanished in the darkness. I made after him on foot, in hopeless and helpless wrath, until he got out of sight. [4]

Roosevelt and his compatriot eventually caught up to the buffalo and feasted on the "uncommonly good" meat from the kill.[5] Despite the thrill he derived from this adventure, Roosevelt still grudgingly admitted that, "[f]rom the standpoint of humanity at large, the extermination of the buffalo has been a blessing."[6]

Today, it might be hard to imagine that a person could write those words and be considered a conservationist—never mind be elected President of the United States. But Roosevelt recognized that there must be a balance between the protection of our natural resources and the utilization of those resources for the benefit of our society. Buffalo competed for food with the cattle and oxen of American farmers and provided Native Americans with a ready supply of meat during fighting with American troops.[7] In

Roosevelt's analysis, the near extinction of the buffalo was necessary for the settlement of the American West by citizens of the United States. And yet, Roosevelt made sure to join with others to preserve the buffalo and set aside huge expanses of wilderness for future generations of Americans to explore.

I've had my own adventure hunting a member of the buffalo family, so I can understand the lure of taking down one of these animals. But to experience the kind of hunt that Roosevelt described, I had to leave American shores and travel to Africa to go head-to-head with the belligerent African or Cape buffalo (*Syncerus caffer*).

Believed by many to be the fiercest, nastiest and most vindictive of the Dark Continent's "Big Five" mature bulls, the Cape buffalo carries an impressive armored boss and heavy curved black horns. Many are the stories of Cape buffalo seeking revenge on their attackers—turning the hunter into the hunted. No amount of prose, however, can prepare a hunter for a close encounter with the famed charge of a wounded Cape buffalo. Facing down the rage of such a beast only served to heighten my respect for the Cape buffalo and for the many hunters and writers who had gone before me into the African bush.

My hunt began with a long trip out of Windhoek, Namibia into the Caprivi Strip (bordering Angola, Zambia and Botswana) and over to Kasika Island across the Chobe River from Botswana. My good friend and professional hunter, Fred Bezentenhuit, and I decided that we would hunt across the broader islands for the first few days to check tracks and spore, so as to determine the routes the buffalo were taking to and from the water holes. Mature bulls seek water once a day, so tracing these paths would increase our chances of success. After making introductions with the "Kuta," the chief of the local tribe, we began a long and difficult hunt, one that would conclude with a face-to-face encounter with one of these cunning and powerful one-ton brutes.

The first two days of scouting gave me the opportunity to observe the diverse wildlife that inhabits the islands. I was treated to the sight of herds of elephants and buffalo, a variety of crocodiles and hippopotami, and countless species of birds (the Caprivi area is famed for more than 300 species of indigenous birds). I found the crocodiles to be particularly ominous because Fred planned to take us through their territory in order to track our buffalo.

It was on the third day of our hunt that we found the fresh tracks of two large bulls. Eager to find these animals, we set forth with great purpose over very daunting geography. At times I began to believe the bulls knew we were following them and tried to lose us in the virtually impassable water channels that were dense with reeds and filled with the overflow from the Chobe River. It reminded me of the thickest black water areas of the Louisiana bayou. The beasts led us across fields covered with tall reed grass over 10 feet high. The wall of reeds made it impossible to see beyond three or four feet; we risked stumbling into one of the Cape buffalo, who lie down in these grasses after wallowing in the mud. The stifling temperatures—over 100 degrees Fahrenheit—only added to the difficulty of our hunt. The thick weeds and intense heat of the African summer made every breath a chore.

We had set out at 7:30 a.m. that morning and tracked these trophy bulls for over eight hours. Finally, we spotted the buffalo across a large reed patch on the other side of another wide channel. To have a chance at a shot, we would have to make it across the channel and into favorable wind without being detected in order to head off the bulls as they made their way to the mud patch.

As we crossed the channel, our luck was holding—the bulls had settled in for a long mud bath. We climbed out of the channel and prepared to get in front of the bulls, when suddenly, they began moving again. Fred and I dropped into a "belly-crawl" and traversed about 50 yards of muddy earth on our stomachs to place ourselves in line for a shot.

Fred motioned me to a halt, indicating he had found a site for a shot. With the calm that comes from his years of experience, Fred stood his shooting sticks, and we waited in the prone position. After a few moments, the bulls stopped momentarily to graze. This was my chance. I stood and lined up for a shot of about 100 yards. Then both the bulls lifted their heads and began to move. I squeezed the trigger on my rifle, and watched with satisfaction as my shot struck the first bull in the chest. The bulls charged off in the opposite direction. Not wanting the wounded animal to get away I fired twice more, striking the beast in the front and back shoulders. Amazingly, the buffalo managed to escape into the tall grass.

Now we were in pursuit of a wounded and ferocious Cape buffalo, who was hiding in terrain in its favor. We swam across another channel carrying our fully reloaded rifles, believing we were ready for anything. But nothing could prepare me for what came next.

The ingenuity of these animals quickly became apparent. The wounded bull ran into the tall reeds, keeping the wind at his back. As we would soon learn, the buffalo had run about 200 yards into the protection provided by the reeds before circling back to stop just before an open area created by game lying down in the mid-day sun.

In approaching the center of this open area, we unknowingly stumbled into the bull's killing zone. I heard a sound on my right and reached out to tap Fred on the shoulder to let him know. As it turned out, Fred did not need my warning because the bull made his presence known just eight yards from where we stood. He launched into a full charge, determined to defend himself. Fred fired the first shot with a 500-grain round from his open-sighted .458. I dropped to one knee and scoped the large bull—a sight I will long remember. As I focused through the scope I was transfixed by the rampaging beast: his eyes red with intensity, the bulk of his massive horns, and his impressive, mammoth body. Fred's hip shot lifted the bull's front feet off the ground, allowing me the perfect shot at his heart, only seven yards from where I knelt. The beast slid to the ground. Out of abundance of caution, Fred followed up with a shot to the animal's spine, to ensure that the bull was down for good.

It is said that a Cape buffalo can achieve a speed of 35 miles per hour. At seven yards, I had less than two seconds to make a shot before the 84-inch bull, weighing over one ton, smashed into me. I have no illusions as to what the results of that encounter would have meant for me: two seconds were all that stood between me and death. And those moments will be forever burned into my memory.

Returning from our successful hunt we shared our kill with the local Kuta and villagers who seemed pleased with all the meat from the buffalo. As for me, I am happy to have enjoyed (and survived) a close encounter with the Cape buffalo, one of the most calculating and lethal animals I have had the pleasure to hunt.

It is a shame that an experience like this is not readily available within the continental United States. Today, "big game" hunting in the United States is often characterized as the hunting of bears, mountain lions, elk and various species of sheep, goat and deer. While each experience is thrilling in its own way, nothing can compare to the adventure in hunting the truly big game of Africa.

And yet, as Roosevelt would surely agree, elephants and lions roaming across Kansas would not be compatible with the lifestyles of modern American society. I mention this because it is important for American outdoorsmen and women to take an active role in preserving our environment in a practical and sensible way. Our goal should be to protect the natural beauty of the land in a way that accommodates and complements our lifestyles; not impose on our society an absolute "hands-off" approach to the outdoors.

America's sportsmen have a long history of taking measures to conserve and protect the nature we enjoy. From the mid-19th century until the early 20th century, sportsmen were the leaders of the American conservation movement. From the early writings of a New York attorney to the conservation laws signed by one of America's most rugged Presidents, our nation's sporting enthusiasts have left their stamp on the American outdoors.

The sensible, proactive approach American sportsmen have taken to preserve our environment is needed to address the most prominent environmental issue of our generation—global climate change. Opinion polls show that anywhere from 70-85 percent of Americans believe that global warming is happening.[8] Our elected leaders are responding to these beliefs by enacting legislation to help address these issues but, oftentimes, are not giving full consideration to the practical implications of the new restrictions they are imposing on our way of life. The challenge we face today is to do something to conserve our environment while maintaining the sensibility that has always been a part of the American spirit—especially that of the American outdoorsmen.

---

[1] "Buffalo-Bison." *National Bison Association*. 2007. U.S. Census Bureau. <http:///www.americanwest.com>.
[2] *Ibid.*
[3] Roosevelt, Theodore. *Hunting Trips of a Ranchman*. New York and London: G.P. Putnam's Sons, 1885.
[4] *Ibid.*
[5] *Ibid.*
[6] *Ibid.*
[7] *Ibid.*
[8] Harris Poll, 16-23 Oct 2007; Associated Press-Stanford University Poll, 21-23 Sep. 2007; FOX News/Opinion Dynamics Poll, 30-31 Jan 2007. <http://www.pollingreport.com/enviro.htm>.

Conservation Takes Root in American Soil

"The practice of conservation must spring from a conviction of what is ethically and aesthetically right, as well as what is economically expedient. A thing is right only when it tends to preserve the integrity, stability, and beauty of the community and the community includes the soil, waters, fauna, and flora, as well as people."
—Aldo Leopold

The birth of the modern conservation movement in the United States is said to have begun in the middle of the 19th century.[9] As more and more people flocked to the cities to make a living, Americans developed a new scientific, philosophical and aesthetic appreciation for nature.[10] America was—and still is—a beautiful country and home to numerous natural resources. It wasn't long, though, before those resources were stripped and wildlife started to disappear. With the population influx in America and the need for natural resources increasing exponentially, the open wilderness was game, literally, for anyone with two hands. But it was most notably the sportsman, exploring the rural frontiers of the country, who noticed the profound changes occurring in our nation's wildernesses and aimed to do something about it.

In 1857, Samuel H. Hammond published what is considered by many to be the first American hunter-as-conservationist book, *Wild Northern Scenes: Sporting Adventures with the Rifle and Rod*. Hammond was a New

York state senator and attorney, whose father founded the village of Hammondsport in western New York. An avid sportsman who spent a great deal of free time in the Adirondack region, Hammond saw the wilderness as "a place where man could truly become one with nature, find his roots, and find rest from life's troubles."[11] He wrote: "Had I my way, I would mark out a circle of a hundred miles in diameter, and throw around it the protecting ægis of the constitution. I would make it a forest forever."[12]

Although Hammond would not live to see it, New York would do exactly that in creating the Adirondack Forest Preserve in 1885. The state also amended its constitution a decade later to require the region to "forever be kept as wild forest lands."[13] His writings inspired sportsmen from across the state to not only come explore the Adirondacks, but to fight for its preservation.

By the mid-1870s, hunters and anglers had formed more than 500 local associations and clubs with the goal of preventing the loss of wildlife and restoring species that had been made nearly extinct.[14] They established a sort of fraternity between themselves and adhered to certain rules of conduct. As serious sportsmen, they would observe gentlemanly behavior in the field, express an aesthetic appreciation for the environment and give their prey a chance for survival.[15] In addition, game would not be sold out of season or for profit and would not be hunted in unreasonable quantities. What separates this class of sportsmen from others is their inherent appreciation for the value and beauty of nature, *and* for the creatures in it. Game would be caught and killed for the challenge of the sport and not acquired through unfair advantages. This meant that hunters and fishermen who observed these guidelines would stalk their prey on a more even playing field without traps and allow the animal an opportunity for escape.

Concern for the environment among hunters and anglers kept growing. Although many seemed to hunt and fish in accordance with these rules of conduct, some did not. Commercial fishermen, for example, were frequently viewed as "cheaters" who used netting to catch fish and did so, oftentimes, out of season. John J. Brown, author of *The American Angler's Guide*, suggested that hunters and anglers merge to pass "strong laws against taking or vending [peddling] game out of season, strictly enforced by the rigorous prosecution of all offenders."[16] Brown also urged sportsmen to form groups regionally and locally to help enforce these statutes and keep their gaming grounds and game preserved. Despite their efforts, however, the general outlook on conservation was grim. The lack of legislation concerning game preservation paired with the public's aversion to the hunting laws presented some obstacles in their quest to improve and protect the land and wildlife.

Shane Mahoney, a conservation biologist and leading authority for the North American Wildlife Conservation Model, explains: "The passionate commitment to resource conservation was matched by an enduring pragmatism that saw grassroots political establishments as a key to long-term success."[17] Making real, lasting changes required awareness at the local level that spanned nationwide, and a genuine concern and interest among Americans to protect their country—not from enemies, but from themselves.

What was needed was for all parties involved—sportsmen *and* non-sportsmen—to understand the implications of what could happen to their environment, their nation and world, if no one took action. In other words, someone needed to draw upon the energy of this grassroots movement and focus it on the national stage.

With the advent of such publications as *Forest and Stream,* *Field and Stream,* and *American Sportsman,* sportsmen were given a voice and a way to communicate across a broader platform. These newspapers came at a time when the conservation movement needed them most. The urbanization and rapid growth in the nation became problematic at best, as far as the environment was concerned. Mass transportation, industrialization and mass-production helped to diminish America's wild landscape into a commercial breeding ground:

> Previously undeveloped regions, teeming with animals, birds, and fish, were made readily accessible to all, and improved guns, ammunition . . . which the average man could afford . . . . Hunting and fishing now became not only more practical, but also more profitable.[18]

Profitability made for a good selling point with some hunters and anglers. The abundance and variety of wildlife paired with the availability and affordability of weapons made hunting a lucrative business for any man or woman who had the time. And while some jumped on the bandwagon with dollar signs in their eyes, others foresaw the dangers of making these sports a commercial endeavor.

Shortly after the Civil War, Charles Hallock became a pioneer in conservation and game management. He advocated the use of proper hunting and fishing methods; forest management; game laws; an industry in fish culture to help revive the fish population; and the development of "domesticating and 'farming' fur-bearing animals."[19] Hallock went on to establish *Forest and Stream* in 1873, a periodical that was one of the most influential publications to come out of the conservation movement during the time. Hallock made it clear that he did not endorse or condone unsportsmanlike behavior and wanted to serve as "an example so compelling as to cause the ignorant and unethical to give up their ways and join the ranks of the initiate."[20] Founded on the principles of what he (and many others like him) considered to be truly sportsmanlike, *Forest and Stream* catered to the *real* sportsman who hunted for pleasure and aesthetic appreciation of nature and game. This kind of sportsman did not look at his quarry as potential income or debase the sport through unfair hunting methods; the real hunter followed the rules of the sport and understood the importance of keeping nature's balance.

Another who understood this dynamic was George Bird Grinnell, an experienced naturalist and businessman, who owned and edited a series of magazines including *American Angler, American Sportsman* and *Forest and Stream* (which he bought from Hallock in 1880). Like Hallock, Grinnell was devoted to promoting "the code of the sportsman," and called for an appropriate appreciation of the natural world.[21] He was focused on how, when and why game was taken and disdained those who hunted out-of-season with illegal methods or for commercial profit.[22] It was Grinnell who served as a leading representative for the American sportsman, bringing the concerns of outdoorsmen to the forefront of the conservation movement.

Grinnel, ca. 1900 [23]

With the encroachment of civilization upon the frontier and the resulting reduction in game populations Grinnell understood the frustration outdoorsmen were experiencing.[24] He, too, realized the potentially hazardous effects industrialization could have on the environment.

The lumber industry, for example, was taking its toll on the environment, especially in New York in the Adirondack region. Deforestation caused a variety of problems for the environment and for sportsmen: large clearings displaced many animal populations; felling trees destroyed saplings, eroded the soil and ruined fishing waters.[25] Keeping with the sportsmen's code, Grinnell maintained that sportsmanship was an essential factor to the sport and to maintaining and protecting the environment. With relentless effort, Grinnell insisted that America was not a "commodity of capitalism"[26] like the mainstream public seemed to believe—it was integral to both the sport and the ecology. His persistence paid off in 1885 when the state of New York established a preserve of more than 700,000 acres.[27]

Needless to say, the concerns that arose due to the pressure of the burgeoning civilization created some dissatisfaction among the nation's naturalists. Grinnell took this unease and organized it into efforts to promote conservation of the nation's resources.[28]

One result of such efforts was the Audubon Society, founded in 1886, which served as the cornerstone for the American wildlife conservation movement. Named after the naturalist, John James Audubon, the Audubon Society was at the time one of the few establishments that had concentrated efforts on the protection of nongame species.

Grinnell used his position at *Forest and Stream* to write editorials appealing to the public to stop the destruction of bird species integral to the ecology. Women, especially were important in this conservation movement. Grinnell urged them to avoid wearing some of the fashion of the day (hats featuring bird feathers and plumes), which tended to indirectly promote the killing of animals, specifically nongame birds like the egret.[29]

Perhaps most important in Grinnell's crusade for game management was his idea of continual and effective administration in protecting habitats and wildlife. His position as editor of *Forest and Stream* put him at an advantage in the fight for proper game management.

While Hallock used his publication to argue for more legislation, Grinnell proposed better enforcement of the laws already in place.[30] To do this, he called on legislators to establish a county game system financed by small fees from the hunters.[31] The officials were to be non-political and enforcement of game laws would be ongoing. The rationale behind it was that enforcement officers could be "free from local pressure, so that their work could be performed efficiently and without interruption."[32]

This innovative idea for enforcement of game laws became the basis for the conservation movement in America.[33] It was also this ideology that sparked the interest of a young Theodore Roosevelt, who eventually paired up with Grinnell, making the two a force to be reckoned with in the American conservation movement.

Grinnell had his first opportunity to speak at length with Theodore Roosevelt after *Forest and Stream* magazine published an unflattering review of Roosevelt's *Hunting Trips of a Ranchman* in 1885.[34] Grinnell, who had accompanied Army expeditions through much of the same area, told the young Roosevelt that his work was more myth than fact, but that it showed a lot of passion for the outdoors.[35] Despite the confrontational nature of their first meeting, the two men grew to be close friends and partners based on their shared love of the wilderness.[36]

Theodore Roosevelt, 1885 [37]

In 1887, Roosevelt joined Grinnell in founding the Boone and Crockett Club.[38] The Club became the first private organization to address the issues of conservation as part of a nationwide agenda.[39] The members set forth the following goals of the organization:

> (1) "To promote manly sport with a rifle."
> (2) "To promote travel and exploration in the wild and unknown, or but partially known, portions of the country." (3) "To work for the preservation of the large game of this country, and, so far as possible, to further legislation for that purpose, and to assist in enforcing the existing laws." (4) "To promote inquiry into, and to record observations on, the habits and natural

> history of the various wild animals." (5) "To bring about among the members the interchange of opinions and ideas on hunting, travel, and exploration; on the various kinds of hunting rifles; on the haunts of game animals, etc."[40]

The sentiment of "fair chase," established in the club's constitution, was the first document of its kind to outline a code of ethics for sportsmen, which later became the cornerstone of the game laws we have today."[41] In line with the ideology behind Hallock and Grinnell's game management plans, the Boone and Crockett Club aimed to remain consistent with the gentleman-like behavior espoused by the club. In addition, the club placed particular emphasis on using, without waste, the game killed and maintaining an effective, continual approach to enforcing legislation.

Originally, the Boone and Crockett Club included only sportsmen who had killed large game. Eventually, however, the members must have seen the benefit in admitting nonsportsmen into their ranks. John W. Noble, for example, was an associate member of the club who admired the sport.

Noble proved highly influential in helping to enact legislation for conservation in 1891 when he urged President Benjamin Harrison to set aside a portion of the Yellowstone National Park to protect the region against mass transportation, poachers and logging. Harrison did and, in doing so, created the first forest reserve, the Yellowstone National Park Timberland Reserve.

The Boone and Crockett Club proved instrumental in raising public and political awareness about the issues facing the environment and wildlife. In 1900, President McKinley signed the Lacey Act, a law introduced by Iowa Representative John F. Lacey that protected wildlife from illegal capture and commercial sale.

The impetus for this bill came from an incident in which a poacher, Edgar Howell, was arrested for killing buffalo in the area. Buffalo, at the time, were bringing in "large sums from taxidermists who hoped to stock up before the species became extinct."[42]

After Grinnell publicized the incident in *Forest and Stream*, the fight for Yellowstone gained momentum as the public grew concerned about the possible extinction of the species. The Lacey Act provided the foundation for present-day laws and established the policy of the National Park Service, formed in 1916.

The act has since been amended several times with a primary focus on preventing introduction of the invasive or non-native species. Poaching nearly caused the buffalo to become extinct. However, it was Grinnell's relentless pursuit for passage of legislation protecting buffalo in Yellowstone that eventually saved the species.

The fight for Yellowstone National Park served as the foundation for the modern American conservation movement. Concern for Yellowstone brought together some of the most powerful and influential leaders of the conservation movement in America. Not only was the region the first of its kind to receive national recognition on an environment-related issue, but "Yellowstone was . . . the birthplace of the national parks and the policy for administering them—it was also the cradle of the forest reserves."[43]

By advocating the continual enforcement of legislation and the wise use of the nation's natural resources, the Boone and Crockett Club helped shape future policies for American land and wildlife conservation, thus becoming the first organization to do so nationally. The founding principles of the Boone and Crockett Club and the ideas it generated over the next two decades would become a vital part of the conservation movement and the policies of the federal government when Theodore Roosevelt later ascended to the office of the President of the United States.

Although he adhered to the sportsmen's code, Roosevelt wasn't originally accepting of the sportsman's responsibility to the environment. But, eventually, his love for hunting developed into a love for the land and a concern for the rapid disappearance of some species. It wouldn't be too long before Roosevelt's and others' concerns would be brought to the table and dealt with in a proactive way. By joining Grinnell's battle to save Yellowstone, Roosevelt started his career as an active conservationist and became an increasingly positive force in the movement.

Grinnell was actually disappointed when Roosevelt agreed to run as vice president with President William McKinley as he sought his second term in office.[44] Roosevelt had just completed his two-year term as New York's governor, during which time he overhauled the state's Fisheries, Game, and Forest Commission with Grinnell's close consultation.[45] Grinnell believed that serving as vice president would be a dead end for

Roosevelt's political career and would deprive the conservation movement of one of its best-placed political allies.[46]

On September 6, 1901, six months after McKinley's second term began, the President was greeting the public at the Pan-American Exposition in Buffalo, New York. As he reached out his hand to welcome a young man named Leon Czolgosz, the President was met with a .32 caliber revolver. Czolgosz fired two shots into McKinley's shoulder and chest. McKinley would die eight days later from his wounds.

Vice President Roosevelt was sworn in as President of the United States on September 14, 1901, in Buffalo. At 42 years old, Roosevelt became the youngest person to serve as President. He turned his energy toward utilizing the power of his position to preserve the nation's wildernesses and maintain the wildlife that filled them. He believed that the:

> . . . qualities of courage, of hardihood, of willingness to face danger, the cultivation of the power of instantaneous decision under difficulties, and the other qualities which go to make up the virile side of a man's character. . . are all-important. . . . No nation can rise to greatness without them.[47]

It is no doubt that George Bird Grinnell had an immeasurable sway over the policies and committees Roosevelt put into place during his administration. The two remained close friends during this time and Grinnell was considered one of his primary advisors concerning the ethics of conservation. In his book, *American Sportsmen and the Origins of Conservation*, John F. Reiger notes that between the years of 1885-97, Roosevelt was like a sponge that absorbed not only Grinnell's ideas but also his point of view.[48]

In his review of Grinnell's ideology, Reiger cites three main themes that are important in understanding the conservation movement and Grinnell's influence on Roosevelt. First, the vulnerability of the earth was perhaps the first indication to Grinnell that the environment was and is not an endless resource; that the land is continually changing. Grinnell reached this conclusion after a dinosaur-hunting expedition with Yale University in 1870 in which he saw, firsthand, the effects of climate changes and evolution.

Secondly, Grinnell's knowledge of the business world paired with his passion for the sport made him an excellent resource in appealing to the masses. By addressing natural resources as something that could be handled like a business, Grinnell communicated to his audiences that these resources could be utilized for several generations without the threat of depletion, if only they were "managed" wisely.

The third theme—and perhaps most important of these themes, according to Reiger—is the sportsman's code of conduct. The sportsman's responsibilities to the environment permeated Grinnell's magazine editorials and, eventually, the ideology caught on among hunters and anglers. The sportsman's code of conduct served as the basis for many fraternities similar to the Boone and

Crockett Club and influenced many major conservation policies during the time.[49]

As a big-game hunter, Roosevelt was convinced that wilderness recreation and hunting were a primary means to maintain the "manhood" of the American citizen in the face of increasing urbanization of the population.[50] He wrote:

> Every believer in manliness, and therefore manly sport, and every lover of nature, every man who appreciates the majesty and beauty of the wilderness and of wild life, should strike hands with the far-sighted men who wish to preserve our material resources, in the effort to keep our forests and our game beasts, game birds, and game fish—indeed, all the living creatures of prairie, and woodland, and seashore—from wanton destruction . . . . But this end can only be achieved by wise laws and by resolute enforcement of our laws.[51]

Roosevelt pursued this vision with great perseverance. For example, in 1903, he visited John Muir in Yosemite, who told Roosevelt about the mismanagement of the park and the continual decline of natural resources. Even before he entered the park, Roosevelt was convinced that the valley needed to be federally managed.

During his two terms as President, Roosevelt created five national parks, four big-game refuges, 51 national bird reservations, 150 national forests and the U.S. Forest

Service, an instrumental agency in managing and enforcing the legislation in accordance with the principles of scientific forestry.

Roosevelt also signed the 1906 Antiquities Act (National Monuments Act), which he then used to designate 18 national monuments.[52] Roosevelt placed approximately 230 million acres of the United States under the protection of the public.[53]

History has remembered Roosevelt as our nation's "Conservationist President" and reminders of his service are visible across the nation. A national park in North Dakota bears his name as well as the Theodore Roosevelt Island Park in Washington, D.C. Three historic sites representative of Roosevelt's life in New York have been set aside in his honor: the Theodore Roosevelt Birthplace National Historic Site; the Sagamore Hill National Historic Site; and the Theodore Roosevelt Inaugural National Historic Site.

Mount Rushmore: Washington, Jefferson, Roosevelt, and Lincoln (left to right)[54]

But perhaps most notable and well-known to all Americans is his place next to George Washington, Thomas Jefferson and Abraham Lincoln on Mount Rushmore in South Dakota.[55]

Roosevelt's mentor and friend, George Bird Grinnell, also is honored by having one of the great glaciers of Glacier National Park in Montana bear his name. Grinnell's connection to the park dates back to 1885 when Grinnell first came to the area.[56] Two years later, he returned to explore and photograph the glaciers at the heads of the Swiftcurrent and Grinnell Valleys.[57] The expedition later named one of these glaciers in his honor.[58]

Grinnell returned numerous times over the years exploring and cataloguing the game animals found in the region.[59] Grinnell would spend the next two decades urging for protection of the lands, culminating in the establishment of Glacier National Park in 1910.[60]

The U.S. Geological Survey (USGS) estimates that in 1850, Grinnell Glacier covered approximately 2.33 square kilometers (about 576 acres) of land.[61] By 1993, the glacier covered less than .88 square kilometers (about 217 acres).[62] USGS predicts that Grinnell Glacier and the other glaciers of the Lewis Range will completely vanish by 2030.[63]

While Roosevelt's face on Mount Rushmore is expected to survive for another 7 million years,[64] some scientists predict that Grinnell Glacier will most likely vanish in the next two decades, and the habitats around these glaciers will change dramatically. Images like these drive public debate on climate change creating pressure on our government to take some action in response.

Grinnell Glacier (covering lake at bottom) from Mt. Gould, 1938-2006 [65]

America's outdoorsmen may have come under scrutiny for alleged insensitivity toward wildlife, but it's clear from history that they have played an essential role in the American conservation movement. And their actions have demonstrated they are anything but insensitive.

Hunters and anglers have fought tooth and nail to preserve the environment and its wildlife, not only for the sake of their sport, but also for the enjoyment of several future generations. They still have a major part to play, too, in continuing the work those before them set out to do.

In addressing issues like climate change and habitat degradation it is critical to draw upon the traditional American values of men like Hallock, Grinnell and Roosevelt and to use our ingenuity and creativity to develop and promote new technologies that preserve the great outdoors for future generations. These technologies should be employed in such a way that complements—not challenges—the pastimes of America's sportsmen and women.

[9] Heckscher, Jurretta Jordan, ed. Preface. *The Evolution of the Conservation Movement, 1850-1920*. Washington, D.C. : Library of Congress, 1996.
[10] *Ibid*.
[11] Hammond, Samuel H. *Wild Northern Scenes: Sporting Adventures with the Rifle and the Rod*. New York: Derby & Jackson, 1857. p.84.
[12] *Ibid*., at 83.
[13] New York State Constitution. Article XIV, sec. 1.
[14] Mahoney, Shane. "The North American Wildlife Conservation Model: Triumph for Man and Nature." *Bugle Magazine* May/June 2004.
[15] Reiger, John F. *American Sportsmen and the Origins of Conservation*. 3. Corvallis: Oregon State University Press, 2001. p.3.
[16] Brown, John J. qtd in *ibid*., at 20.
[17] Mahoney *supra* n.14.
[18] Reiger *supra* n. 15 at 47.
[19] *Ibid*. at 50.
[20] *Ibid*.
[21] *Ibid*.
[22] *Ibid*. at 52.
[23] *George Bird Grinnell*. Photograph. circa 1900. Ruthven Deane Collection, New York. *The Harriman Expedition Retraced*. 2008. Public Broadcasting Service (PBS). <http://www.pbs.org/harriman/1899/1899_part/participantgrinnell.html>.
[24] Bird, Jillian L. "George Bird Grinnell." *Minnesota State University Emuseum*. <http://www.mnsu.edu/emuseum/information/biography/fghij/grinnell_george_bird.html>.
[25] Reiger *supra* n. 15 at 111.
[26] *Ibid*. at 54.
[27] *Ibid*. at 118.
[28] Bird *supra* n.24.
[29] Reiger *supra* n.15 at 93.
[30] *Ibid*.
[31] *Ibid*.
[32] *Ibid*.
[33] *Ibid*. at 93.
[34] Mahoney, Shane. "George Bird Grinnell: The Father of American Conservationism Part 2." *Bugle Magazine*. Jan./Feb. 2005.

35 *Ibid.*
36 *Ibid.*
37 Baine, George Grantham. *Theodore Roosevelt, full-length portrait, facing front, in deer skin hunting suit, rifle in hands.* Photograph. 1885. Library of Congress Prints and Photographs Division, Washington, D.C. *Portraits of the Presidents and First Ladies, 1789-Present.* Library of Congress. <http://lcweb2.loc.gov/cgi-bin/query/r?ammem/presp:@field%28NUMBER+@band%28cph+3a24199%29%29>.
38 Reiger *supra* n. 15 at 151.
39 *Ibid.*
40 *Ibid.*
41 "History of the Boone and Crockett Club: The Legacy." *The Boone and Crockett Club.* 2008. The Boone and Crockett Club. < http://www.boone-crockett.org/about/about_overview.asp?area=about>.
42 Reiger *supra* n. 15 at 162.
43 *Ibid.* at 173.
44 *Ibid.* at 180.
45 *Ibid.* at 175-9.
46 *Ibid.* at 180.
47 Theodore Roosevelt. "Remarks to the Young Men's Christian Association." Topeka. 01 May 1903.
48 Reiger *supra* n. 15 at 181.
49 *Ibid.* at 182.
50 Filler, Daniel. "Theodore Roosevelt: Conservation as the Guardian of Democracy." *Yale University.* 28 Dec 1995. <http://pantheon.cis.yale.edu/~thomast/essays/filler/filler.html>.
51 "Notes and Literature: Zoology." *The American Naturalist.* Boston: Ginn & Co. Publishers, Sep 1902.
52 Filler *supra* n.50.
53 "Theodore Roosevelt." The Theodore Roosevelt National Park. *National Park Service.* <http://www.nps.gov/archive/thro/tr_cons.htm>.
54 *Mount Rushmore.* Photograph. *Ben's Guide to U.S. Government for Kids.* 31 Jan. 2008. U.S. Government Printing Office. 20 Aug. 2008 <http://bensguide.gpo.gov/3-5/symbols/mountrushmore.html>.
55 *Ibid.*

56 Robinson, Donald H. *Through the Years in Glacier National Park: An Administrative History*. Glacier National History Association, 1960.
57 *Ibid.*
58 *Ibid.*
59 *Ibid.*
60 *Ibid.*
61 Fagre, Daniel B., Carl H. Key, and Richard K. Menicke. "Glacier Retreat in Glacier National Park, Montana." *Satellite Image Atlas of Glaciers of the World, Glaciers of North America - Glaciers of the Western United States*. Eds. R.S. Williams, Jr. and J.G. Ferrigno. Washington D.C.: United States Government Printing Office, 2002. p.J365-J381
62 *Ibid.*
63 "Glacier Monitoring Studies: Monitoring and Assessing Glacier Changes and Their Associated Hydrologic and Ecologic Effects in Glacier National Park." *Northern Rocky Mountain Science Center*. 24 Jul 2008. U.S. Department of Interior & The U.S. Geological Survey. <http://www.nrmsc.usgs.gov/research/glaciers.htm>.
64 Weisman, Alan. *The World Without Us*. Thomas Dunne Books, 2007.
65 Hileman, T.J., courtesy Glacier National Park Archives, 1939; Carl Key, courtesy U.S. Geological Survey, 1981; Dan Fagre, courtesy U.S. Geological Survey,1998; Karen Holzer, courtesy U.S. Geological Survey, 2006. Grinnell Glacier from Mt. Gould 1938-2006. *Northern Rocky Mountain Science Center*. 24 Jul 2008. U.S. Department of Interior & U.S. Geological Survey. <http://www.nrmsc.usgs.gov/repeatphoto/gg_mt-gould.htm>.

THE GROWTH OF MODERN CONSERVATION

"In wildness is the preservation of the world."
— Henry David Thoreau

It's been more than a century since the American conservation movement grew from a grassroots movement to mainstream consciousness, and along the way, defined key components of federal and state government policies.

The idea of wildlife and habitat conservation was eagerly embraced by the sportsmen of early America, who aimed to protect the land for future generations and for the sake of their sport. The code of conduct sportsmen developed and followed has served as the foundation for many of the wildlife protection efforts pursued in North America over the 20th century and still continues to influence the conservation movement today.[66]

As discussed in the previous chapter, these guidelines helped secure the role hunters and anglers played in the environmental movements in their respective sports. Essential to the code was that sportsmen must be gentlemen in the field.

Conduct of the gentlemen hunter entailed pursuing their game legally and without traps, so as to allow their prey a fair chance to evade the hunter. In addition, taken game was to be utilized to the fullest extent without waste and was not to be sold for commercial profit.

This hunter's code eventually expanded to include the protection of non-game species (in order to maintain the ecological habitat of game species) as well as the sportsman's responsibility to nature and to ensure the continuation of the sport.[67]

The modern North American model for wildlife management is unique in that it has evolved to see fish and wild game as a public resource and to manage that resource scientifically with the assistance of hunters.[68] In Europe, by contrast, hunting is dependent on landowners, who lease land for hunting, and are responsible for managing the wildlife on their particular parcels of land.[69] The American system has largely prevented the wide scale adoption of efforts to commercialize the harvesting of game, as in game ranching and fee hunting.[70]

Seven features of the North American Conservation Model contribute to our unique system of game management:

1. Wildlife is a public resource. This notion dates back to the Bible and the legal codes of ancient Rome. No one owned a wild animal until it was physically possessed. The concept was solidified in the United States to the extent that wildlife was held in common ownership by the state for the benefit of all people.
2. Markets for trade in wildlife were eliminated in the early 1900s with the Lacey Act. The act made it illegal to buy and sell meat and parts of game and nongame species, removing a huge threat to sustaining those species. At the same time, how-

ever, allowing markets for furbearers have helped manage them as a sustainable resource, in conjunction with restrictive regulations and advocacy of trappers for land stewardship.
3. Allocation of wildlife by law. States allocate surplus wildlife by law, not by market pressures, land ownership or special privilege. The public gets a say in how wildlife resources are distributed; the process fosters public involvement in managing wildlife.
4. Wildlife can only be killed for a legitimate purpose. The law prohibits killing wildlife for frivolous reasons. Under the "Code of the Sportsman," hunters must use as much of the kill as they can. The harvest of wild animals must serve a practical purpose if society is going to accept it as sport.
5. Wildlife species are considered an international resource. Some species, such as migratory birds, transcend boundaries. One country's management can easily affect a species in another country.
6. Science is the proper tool for discharge of wildlife policy. This is a key concept of wildlife management. It has its roots in the Prussian Forestry System, arising in the United States as the basis of wildlife management by the convincing forcefulness of Theodore Roosevelt and Aldo Leopold. By

spawning the profession of wildlife management, North Americans were decades ahead of their global neighbors.
7. The democracy of hunting. In the European model, wildlife was allocated by land ownership and privilege. In North America, any sportsman in good standing may participate.[71]

Shane Mahoney, a conservation biologist with the Newfoundland and Labrador Wildlife Division, asserts that these concepts of the sportsman's code serve as the basis for many modern habitat and wildlife management efforts. Without these basic principles, the movement in the United States "would be a hodgepodge of conflicting programs that could only culminate in a patchwork of few successes and many failures."[72]

Of these seven concepts, two principles have emerged as the drivers of American conservation. The first is that wildlife should not be killed for commercial profit. The second is that "personal access to wildlife should be restricted to methods, means and purposes that support wise, sustainable use of the resource, in perpetuity," meaning that sportsmen should be, in part, responsible for the wildlife and habitat by way of their hunting methods.[73] Consideration for the land, especially, has always been an important element of the sport, as noted by John F. Reiger, a history professor at Ohio University-Chillicothe and author of *American Sportsmen and the Origins of Conservation*:

> Possessing an Old World code, they saw forests not as a challenge to the American mission of progress, but as one of the essential settings for that important activity called sport. . . . Woodlands were both the home of their quarry and the aesthetic backdrop for that avocation that many considered more rewarding—in a noneconomic sense—than their vocation.[74]

Protecting the lands that support the game has been as critical to sportsmen as protecting the game itself.

Just as sportsmen launched the American conservation movement, they became the leaders and innovators behind the growth of the movement in the early 1900s. Their influence and support was far- and wide-reaching as their organizations and publications voiced distress over the declining state of the nation's wildernesses. Clearly, the North American Conservation Model is reliant upon the strong participation of our sportsmen and women. However, as the conservation movement matured into what many call the "environmental movement," the important role of America's outdoorsmen and women was forgotten.

It's difficult to say when exactly the perceived split occurred between sportsmen and "environmentalists." While some may view hunting and fishing as exploitation, the roles of the hunter and angler in keeping the ecological balance in nature are essential. Moreover, our short cultural memory allows many to forget that sportsmen were the first conservationists and have traditionally been at the forefront in supporting regulation to protect America's wildernesses.

One possible explanation for the divide that emerged between sportsmen and environmentalists centers on the relationship between John Muir, the founder of the Sierra Club, and the Roosevelt administration. Muir is perhaps most notable for his contributions to the Yosemite Valley and Sierra Nevada regions. After first visiting the area in the late 1860s, Muir found himself captivated by the ranges and the serenity of the natural world.

In contrast, Muir was also left disturbed by the destruction of the forests as a result of industrialization:

> . . . entire townships in the East and Midwest had been stripped of the choicest pine and hardwoods, and the soil had been eroded to bare granite . . . By the time Muir reached California, cattle and sheep had grazed the Yosemite Valley down to the dirt, displacing deer, elk, and other wildlife.[75]

As a lover of science, Muir spent countless hours studying the land and making conclusions as to how these habitats were formed. He created inventions that made good use of the land as it was. For example, he constructed a water-powered mill to cut fallen trees and later built himself a cabin.

Muir was passionate about keeping the region pristine and natural. He lobbied relentlessly for the preservation of the area. With the help of Robert Underwood Johnson, associate editor of *Century* magazine, Muir fought to get legislation passed that would protect Yosemite.[76] His efforts came to fruition in September of 1890, when Congress made Yosemite into a national park.

In 1903, Muir was visited in Yosemite by President Theodore Roosevelt as part of the President's increasing interest and activity in the conservation movement. Muir told Roosevelt about the mismanagement of the park and the continual decline of natural resources. Roosevelt was moved by Muir's love of the land and was convinced that the valley needed to be federally managed.

Muir and the serenity of Yosemite [77]

It's possible that without Muir's persistence, Yosemite Valley would not have become a protected area until much later—if at all. In addition, the collaborations between Muir and Roosevelt strengthened the American conservation movement that the Roosevelt administration was putting into effect. While Muir was no longer a hunter by the time he settled in the region, his ideals are reminiscent of the sportsman's code of responsibility and accountability in nature. Roosevelt enjoyed the hunt of big game but he also had an aesthetic appreciation for nature, much like Muir, and would have been just as captivated by the majestic ranges.

Perhaps one of Muir's most notable contributions to the American conservation movement was the establishment of the Sierra Club in 1892. Muir became the first president of the organization and remained so until his death in 1914. Founded on the ideas of exploration, preservation and enjoyment of the natural world, the Sierra Club called on the public to help protect the environment and promoted the wise use of natural resources. The Sierra Club has persisted for more than 115 years, with chapters across the nation, working on numerous conservation issues that span from pollution and waste management to wildlife conservation.

Muir is most often noted for his role as an environmentalist, but it's also important to remember that he was once a hunter as well:

> Though he'd hunted as a young man, Muir had given it up by the time he reached California. He had become personally uncomfortable with the taking of a life; but he still ate meat and regarded hunting as natural and necessary. He viewed humanity's predatory place as a grand, interconnected system, 'Plants, animals and stars are all kept in place, bridled along appointed ways, with one another, and through the

midst of one another—killing and being killed, eating and being eaten, in harmonious proportions and quantities.'[78]

What then caused the rift in the seemingly strong coalition between sportsmen and other environmentally-concerned groups?

Some attribute the divide to John Muir, himself, and fellow conservationist, Gifford Pinchot. By the time Muir met Pinchot in July of 1896, Pinchot was a Yale graduate who had recently returned from a stint in Europe studying forestry.[79] Muir was a member of the Forestry Commission, a division of the National Academy of Sciences. Both were interested in protecting American forests and their commonality ignited a friendship but their opposing viewpoints caused friction, cracking the foundation of the movement they were trying to propel forward.

Muir promoted the aesthetics and human enjoyment of the forests while, at the same time, he encouraged wise use for sustainable and continual growth. Pinchot, on the other hand, fresh from his trip abroad, had been influenced by the Prussian forestry system and argued for a "scientifically prescribed sustained yield approach."[80]

It is possible that they could have set aside their differences had it not been for the Forest Management Act of June 1897, which opened all forest reserves to timber harvesting, mining and grazing.[81]

Pinochet was an advocate of allowing sheep to graze the lands, a practice that Muir condemned, arguing the grazing was especially destructive. The passage of the Act was a defeat for Muir and served to convince him that forests and other natural habitats should be protected independently and not simply as part of a broader agenda.[82]

A number of other factors may have contributed to the tension, including "the emergence of the animal-rights movement, [and] a growing number of urban and suburban Americans, with little experience of farms or slaughterhouses, [who] came to view hunting as backward or barbaric."[83]

The lack of experience with the land may be attributed to the country's movement away from agricultural living and toward urbanization. Americans, after living in the cities long enough, had grown to forget their connection to the land, and some of their "most highly prized values and rituals."[84] The result, more often than not, was a negative attitude toward sportsmen, with inaccurate portrayals of hunters and anglers exploiting animals unable to defend themselves.

In fact, sportsmen were doing the opposite as they continued to be at the forefront of wildlife protection efforts. In 1941, the Kodiak National Wildlife Refuge was established after hunters lobbied for the creation of it to "protect the natural feeding and breeding range of the brown bears and other wildlife" on Kodiak Island, Alaska, and the neighboring islands.

The 1.9-million acre refuge is now home to a variety of wildlife and plant species, but the Kodiak bear is perhaps its most notable figure.[85] Hunters understand the importance of the Kodiak bear to the region and to the nation. There are only about 3,500 Kodiak bears in existence, and they live exclusively on the Kodiak Archipelago in southern Alaska.[86]

Kodiak bears have been isolated on the island chain for more than 12,000 years, so their prominence in the region is widespread and their survival is vital to the local ecology. Kodiak bears are the largest bears in the world. Kodiak males stand over 10 feet tall and can weigh up to 1,500 pounds. Throughout the 1800s, the bears were hunted for their pelts. Toward the beginning and middle of the 20th century, however, farmers and ranchers killed the bears to protect their cattle from attack.

Me and my Kodiak in April of 2008

Fortunately, bear-control efforts stopped in the mid-1960s as the bear population dwindled to smaller and smaller numbers. The decrease in numbers prompted sportsmen of the time to petition for the Kodiak's protection. Tight hunting restrictions limit permit availability allowing the bear population to remain stable and giving serious sportsmen the opportunity to get their big game. Approximately 5,000 resident hunters apply for the near 500 permits available to them each season, while out-of-state hunters can pay up to $21,000 just for the chance at one of these august creatures.[87]

While differences in opinion may have gotten us here—what's more important is what comes next: How can hunters and environmentalists once again work together to forge a united front? Hunters and anglers make up about 20% of the Sierra Club's membership—a little more than 180,000 members—according to Jon Schwedler, the national organizer of Sierra Sportsmen, a division of the Sierra Club. While their group may be small compared to the 600,000 non-sportsmen environmentalists who claim membership in the club, sportsmen should not be disregarded based on their numbers—they are a vital force in the conservation movement. [88]

In efforts to mend the differences between the groups, the Sierra Club is recognizing the growing importance of its hunters and anglers. With its new Sierra Sportsmen website, sportsmen can better express their issues and concerns on a more accessible stage. The Sierra Club launched the site in early May 2008, but there has already been great demand for information from the new resource.

The Sierra Club 2008 platform consists of four major concerns in relation to the sports and the environment: clean water; sporting for kids; sustainable, resilient habitats for wildlife; and protecting Alaska's Teshekpuk Lake.[89]

Perhaps one of the most important projects is the construction of resilient habitats to help combat the effects of climate change. With the help of conservation biologists, the Sierra Sportsmen are pushing efforts to aid in wildlife survival.

The success of the conservation movement is contingent upon the cooperation between sportsmen and environmentalists. Without one another for support, the efforts of each group are stunted. The sportsmen of the Rocky Mountain Elk Foundation (RMEF) and the representatives of The Nature Conservancy serve as a great example of what happens when two seemingly opposing groups put their heads together to come up with a solution.

The hunters of the RMEF number slightly less than the Sierra Sportsmen, but at 150,000 members, they are a strong force in conservation.[90] In 2005, both The Nature Conservancy and the Elk Foundation members combined their efforts to protect more than 800,000 acres of grassland of the Tallgrass Aspen Parklands region in Kittson County, Minnesota. The area is home to numerous wildlife species such as the rare yellow railbird, the Giant Sandhill Crane, the moose, and the black bear.[91]

The Elk Foundation also teamed up with the Conservation Fund and the Wild Turkey Federation in 2003 to save the Tennessee Cumberland Mountain region. The area was in danger of being sold and commercialized. The partnerships came together to protect more than 75,000 acres of forest.[92]

It wasn't merely the interests of sportsmen that saved the territory from deforestation and fragmentation. All groups fighting for protection of wilderness areas—Sierra Club, Nature Conservancy, Elk Foundation and Wild Turkey Federation to name a few—had an investment in the environment that compelled them to fight for its protection. America's sportsmen can rely on their environmentalist counterparts to help with rallying public support, integrating environmental policies with grassroots efforts, and identifying key legal, political and media issues. Similarly, environmentalists need sportsmen, too, for their "deep knowledge of a particular place and ability to speak a language that resonates locally."[93]

The knowledge and ability sportsmen possess make them a motivating and powerful force in the conservation movement. More importantly, however, is the fact that their investment in wildlife and land has been consistent and unwavering since the movement began. Together, these groups can provide convincing arguments to urge the government to act in response to the needs of preserving America's wilderness.

Government Action

In addition to the Lacey Act of 1900, the early part of the century was marked by a period of landmark legislation in conservation that still serves as a strong foundation for similar efforts today. When the Lacey Act failed to stop interstate shipments by market hunters, Congress enacted the Weeks-McLean Act of 1913 to put an end to commercial hunting and illegal migratory bird transportation.

The Weeks-McLean Act, too, failed to deliver results and was replaced by the Migratory Bird Treaty Act in 1918. This legislation protected all migratory birds including their nests, eggs, and feathers. Moreover, the Migratory Bird Treaty Act works in accordance with international convention provisions with Canada, Russia, Japan, and

Mexico to protect birds that are common to the five countries.[94] In 1985, the U.S. Fish & Wildlife Service revised the list of protected birds to extend it to nearly 1,000 protected bird species.[95]

One major contribution sportsmen have made to wildlife and conservation legislation has been the implementation of Duck Stamps. Otherwise known as the Migratory Bird Hunting and Conservation Stamp Act, the Duck Stamp Act is integral to wetlands conservation and has had a major impact on environmental efforts.

Signed in 1934 by President Franklin D. Roosevelt, the Duck Stamp Act requires waterfowl hunters more than 16 years of age to possess a hunting stamp. Since the program's establishment Duck Stamps have generated more than $650 million dollars and have helped purchase more than five million acres of land to be protected under the National Wildlife Refuge System.

The Nature Conservancy recorded that in 2002-2003, Duck Stamps brought in nearly $26 million.[96] About 98 cents of every dollar goes toward the purchase or lease of wildlife habitats and the animals in them including mammals, amphibians, waterfowl, reptiles, and fish. It's estimated that more than one-third of the nation's endangered species population finds protection in the areas purchased by the program. Duck Stamps have proven valuable and beneficial not only for sportsmen but also for conservationists, educators, birders, and collectors.[97]

In an annual report for Fiscal Year 2005, the U.S. Fish & Wildlife Service estimated that approximately 225,000 acres of land were purchased as part of the National Wildlife Refuge (NWR) System. The report cites that these acres were not only used to establish new refuge systems but were added onto previously existing ones. For example, the department teamed up with The Conservation Fund to acquire more than 1,000 acres of land in the lower Cane River region of Louisiana to add to the Red River NWR. The refuge serves as the "cornerstone for restoration of fish and wildlife habitats on this 280-mile stretch of the river." The Nature Conservancy also helped attain 4,362 acres for the Cache River NWR in the Lower Mississippi River Valley region. The refuge is considered to be vital for waterfowl protection and migration in addition to being an important portion of the bottomland hardwood forest of the valley. An interesting discovery of the Ivory-Billed Woodpecker, a bird thought to be extinct, emphasizes how crucial these habitats are to wildlife and the benefits land acquisition has to science, conservation, and the environment.[98]

Waterfowl of the Prairie Pothole region[99]

A major achievement from these partnerships was the addition of a new refuge unit, the Glacial Ridge NWR in

Minnesota. Comprised of 2,309 acres, the Glacial Ridge NWR rests on the edge of the Prairie Pothole Region, located in the Northern Great Plains, and is a prime resource for the study of migratory waterfowl and their habitats.[100] The Prairie Pothole Region stretches across five states, into three Canadian territories, and is considered to be the "Duck Factory" of North America.[101]

This area is the focus of the Emergency Wetlands Loan Act, a bill that aims to further amend the Duck Stamp Act by giving even more protection to the area. While Duck Stamps contribute a great deal by way of land conservation, the proceeds aren't likely to be sufficient in the long run. This new legislation would provide a $400 million advance for Duck Stamp profits in the next ten years, giving conservation efforts a much needed push in concern to land acquisition as "1.4 million acres of high priority 'at risk' wetlands and 10.4 million acres of high priority grasslands are still in need of protection."[102]

These "at risk" lands are some of the best waterfowl breeding grounds in the nation but are being turned over for agricultural production due to increased land values, increased demand for bio-fuels, and higher commodity prices. For example, approximately 820,000 acres of the Conservation Reserve Program were lost in Montana and the Dakotas in 2007.[103] Additionally, the National Land Trust Census Report of 2005 recorded that 2.2 million acres of land are subject to human development each year.[104]

While industry tends to be a sticking point with many concerned environmentalists, animal-rights advocates, and sportsmen, it is important to have a well-rounded view on the efforts corporations are making to ensure economic *and* environmental success. Take for example the Trans-Alaskan Pipeline System (TAPS), the most ambitious construction project in American history. The 800-mile long pipeline system crosses three mountain passes, 500 rivers and streams, four different vegetation regions in Alaska's unspoiled wilderness. Because the project involved such vast areas of public lands, the proposed pipeline required federal construction permits. These applications fueled vigorous public debate from 1969 to 1973 that was unprecedented in American environmental history.[105]

The pipeline eventually was approved and completed in 1977. Since then, more than 15 billion gallons of crude have passed through the pipeline without any major environmental incidents. While environmentalists argued that the above-ground pipeline would hinder the migratory routes of the indigenous caribou, the oil companies incorporated 579 animal crossings into the pipeline to protect wildlife affected by the massive structure.[106]

Established in 1960 by President Dwight Eisenhower, Alaska National Wildlife Refuge (ANWR) covers approximately 19 million acres and is home to a variety of plant and animal life particular only to the region; it is one of the last truly pristine places in North America.[107] Environmentalists express concern that oil spills, production, and development will disturb migrating caribou and hurt the essence of the native habitat. Without a doubt, the refuge and surrounding regions are environmentally significant, but they also hold much economic importance as our nation increasingly relies upon foreign oil resources.

Many fail to realize that stakeholders' concerns reach far beyond the 6 to 16 billion barrels of oil lying beneath the Arctic National Wildlife Refuge (ANWR) and nearby Prudhoe Bay.[108]

Since the pipeline system was built more than 30 years ago, companies have implemented newer, more eco-friendly strategies and technologies to curb the disadvantages of drilling. In designing the system, developers considered caribou migration, stability of permafrost, and earthquake fault lines. Keeping these issues in mind, developers built an elevated, insulated system between five and 15 feet off the ground to prevent the permafrost foundation from thawing. The elevation of the pipeline aided in stability both vertically and laterally because it allowed for movement in case of an earthquake; in 2002, it withstood a 7.9 earthquake along the Denali fault.[109]

Caribou migration is high on the list of concerns, as the animals are a source of subsistence for local natives and are "treasured as a natural wonder of state, national, and international importance."[110] The elevated pipelines allow for herds to travel relatively undisturbed to their migration destinations. There have been few observed individual migration failures and the system has not prohibited caribou population growth dramatically. The biggest foreseeable problem is the potential for oil spills. To remedy this, the pipeline is built with leak protection and monitoring systems, and containment sites. Personnel are also taught how to properly respond to an oil spill and how to manage and interact with the environment, including wildlife.[111]

Despite the success of the pipeline at delivering economic benefits in an environmentally sustainable fashion, there are still many environmental and animal-rights groups who vehemently oppose the pipeline and the proposed drilling in ANWR. There are certainly other methods to transport the oil but none seem nearly as effective for both the economy and the environment:

> The Alaskan Pipeline is a model for sustainable development. It was designed with economic efficiency as well as environmental safety in mind . . . . It may not be the most efficient method, but it is one of the safest ways environmentally . . . the pipeline is the most sustainable method of transporting the oil. The environmentally conscious fashion in which the pipeline was designed is a good paradigm for future development.[112]

The environmental success of a particular region is reflective of the cooperation of those involved. In 2005, Minnesota Public Radio aired a story outlining the decline in success of the duck hunting season. Hunters complained that there were no ducks to hunt in previous years and the scarcity of bird species caused concern among local hunters and citizens. While unusually hotter fall seasons may be a cause for this, the more likely reason may be degradation of the habitat and water quality.

At the time of the broadcast, the Department of Natural Resources cited approximately 11,000 acres of Minnesota wetlands that had been removed with only 6,000 of those acres having been replaced. The problem in losing historic wetlands is significant for the state of Minnesota *and* for the wildlife involved. Furthermore, the radio story noted that whenever wetlands are removed "more runoff is diverted to the remaining wetlands, which are getting deeper, muddier, and weedier and less inviting to ducks."[113]

While some developers replace the wetlands they remove, others don't and aren't required to do so. But regardless, the duck population is suffering for the inconsistencies and, correspondingly, hunters and environmentalists are hurting as well. In a region where duck species were abundant, only three highly adaptable species remain: the mallard, the blue wing teal, and the wood duck.[114] The loss of habitat may also be due to the lack of financial and land incentives for private property owners, like farmers, who often preserve their land for wildlife and conservation initiatives.

Legislators seem to be listening. Sportsmen, environmentalists, politicians, and non-hunters alike are sounding the bell on this issue and giving support to legislation like the Emergency Wetlands Loan Act. Some landowners, for example, are lining up to donate their land for the benefit of the environment. With conservation easements not only do landowners get to help with local conservation efforts but they also get income, estate, and property tax incentives. These agreements give particular non-profit or governmental agencies permanent rights over the land and limit the use of the land for specific conservation values.[115] According to the Land Trust Alliance, a yearly average of 2.6 million acres are protected from conservation easements and local concentrated efforts. Their 2005 report cited that, in five years, the number of acres under protection increased by 148 percent from 2,514,566 in 2000 to 6,245,969 in 2005.[116]

In the Prairie Pothole Region, more than 200,000 acres of land are being offered by local farmers and ranchers at a value of more than $60 million (consistent with 2006 land values) to help protect waterfowl habitats.[117] While these efforts have immeasurable benefits to conservation programs, increases in property values have caused a rise in the costs of easements making them more difficult to attain. In recent years, funding has been insufficient to compensate for the land prices. Conservation organizations like Delta Waterfowl and Ducks Unlimited are calling for an increase in the price of Duck Stamps in addition to the Emergency Wetlands Loan Act. The hike in cost would go from $15 to $25, allowing for nearly 7,000 additional protected acres and securing easements for almost 10,000 acres, and would be the first increase of its kind since 1991.[118] Joseph Satrom of the Great Plains Region of Ducks Unlimited, noted that, even though the bills currently in place are beneficial to conservation efforts, "there continues to be a net loss of habitat for waterfowl and other wildlife and increased resources are needed . . . to ensure these essential habitats for wildlife are not lost forever."[119]

While conservation easements may give individuals tax breaks, other acts of legislation, like the Pittman-Robertson Act of 1937, increased taxes on particular goods in order to benefit the environment. Also known as the Federal Aid to Wildlife Restoration Act, the Pittman-

Robertson Act was introduced by Senator Key Pittman of Nevada and called for an 11 percent tax to be placed on hunting equipment and ammunition. Since then, proceeds have totaled more than $5 billion and have been vital in providing and maintaining wildlife habitats.[120] Funding for conservation projects also came from the Dingell-Johnson Act of 1950, or the Federal Aid in Sport Fish Restoration Act, which provided financing for fish restoration and management plans. This act was amended later with the Wallup-Breaux Act, which extended provisions to expand revenue sources giving more money to state projects, programs, and research for fisheries.[121]

Similar to these bills, State Wildlife Grants borrow the basics from both the Pittman-Robertson and the Dingell-Johnson Acts for cost-effective methods for preventing the endangerment of at-risk species. Originally set as a temporary resolution to the Conservation and Reinvestment Act (commonly known as CARA), the wildlife grants assist with the development and implementation of educational and conservation programs that will benefit wildlife and their habitats. In 2000-2001 the U.S. House of Representatives passed the CARA Act with overwhelming support but the bill remained stagnant with no vote from the Senate.[122] Opponents argued that CARA would have established a permanent fund of more than $1 billion for "land acquisition and condemnation of private property in the name of protecting the environment."[123] Had it been passed, CARA would have expanded parks and recreational areas, protected wildlife and endangered species, and preserved historic buildings. In addition, it would have allocated $3.1 billion a year for conservational needs until 2015.[124]

The CARA act was good in theory, but the State Wildlife Grants have done something new for the environment: they addressed the need of having *preventative* measures to protect wildlife before they become endangered. Through research and carefully monitored species reintroduction, the scientists and conservationists associated with the grants help support a sustainable environment where wildlife can thrive. Furthermore, State Wildlife Grants encourage the proper management of land and land-use and are considered a major source of funding for state- and locally-based conservation projects.[125]

Another source for conservation funding came from the reauthorization of the Farm Bill in 2008, a bill that rewarded companies and citizens who address conservation issues. Private landowners, for instance, were offered tax incentives to encourage the protection of endangered species on their land. Farmers and ranchers benefited from incentives provided by the Environmental Quality Incentives Program (EQIP), an organization that received nearly $2.4 billion from the bill, for their environmental and wildlife conservation efforts.[126] By aiding organizations like EQIP, the new Farm Bill may have encouraged more organizations and individuals to deliver environmentally positive results before it's too late.

Strongly supported by sportsmen, the Farm Bill also created a new initiative, the Open Fields Program, encouraging the use of private land for public use by sportsmen. Introduced by Congressional Sportsmen's

Caucus member Senator Kent Conrad of North Dakota and Senator Pat Roberts of Kansas, Open Fields was designed to enhance pre-existing state programs that call for sportsmen's access to private lands and the improvement of wildlife habitats by the utilization of better management methods. With a $50 million funding source from the bill, Open Fields benefits both sportsmen *and* landowners. With incentives offered to landowners who improve on the quality of their land for wildlife and who voluntarily allow sportsmen to access their property, this group brings together the private landowner and the sportsmen, promoting better habitat management and providing community benefits.[127]

But what's beneficial for the overall community may be challenging to individuals, especially where wildlife is concerned. Take for example a recent conflict surrounding the double-crested cormorant, found primarily in the Great Lakes region of the United States and Canada. The double-crested cormorant is one of several species of cormorant that are known for their somewhat invasive presence. Found anywhere between Southwest Alaska and the Gulf of Mexico these birds are known for causing damage to the aquaculture industry, water quality, game fish populations, and other bird species.[128]

In April 2004 four national and state organizations filed a lawsuit demanding better methods of control over the cormorant population. This was in response to an October 2003 hearing in which the U.S. Fish and Wildlife Service and the U.S. Department of Agriculture called for more flexibility in culling the population in 24 states.[129] The uproar over the birds came after nearly thirty years of steady growth. In the 1950's some were concerned about the decline in cormorant numbers after finding that the birds were eating fish contaminated with the toxins DDT (dichlorodiphenyltrichloroethane) and PCBs (polychlorinated biphenyls). These chemicals, particularly DDT, cause the thinning of eggshells. When DDT enters the body another chemical, DDE (dichlorodiphenyldichloroethylene), is produced. DDE inhibits the production of calcium carbonate, an element necessary for successful cormorant reproduction. The lack of calcium carbonate in the shell resulted in a high mortality rate for nestlings.[130]

The Double-Crested Cormorant[131]

After the 1970's, however, the average annual growth rate for cormorants reached around 35 percent, nearly tripling the population every three years. This was, in part, due to the ban on products using DDT up until 1990.[132] The cormorant population has since exploded up to nearly 600,000 creating mixed reactions among residents in the Great Lakes region. Many are calling for the controlled culling of the species to deter the loss of game fish and other native bird species, while wildlife groups are arguing against such actions because the birds are protected under the 1916 Migratory Bird Treaty. The Canadian Wildlife Service's Ontario Region, however, heralds the cormorant population and views it as a success:

> There is a biological principle that states that the greater the number of different organisms an area can support, i.e. the more diverse the wildlife, the better the area. This is known as biodiversity. The richest areas in the world for biodiversity are the tropics . . . moist, warm areas . . . . The temperate zone areas . . . where the Great Lakes are located, are comparatively poor in biodiversity . . . . We have lost many species from the Great Lakes already . . . we don't need to lose anymore.[133]

As the climate changes, it will impact the double crested cormorant and other species. Focusing on the Great Lakes region in particular, climate change has started to affect almost every area of the environment. The region is one that is most altered by human interference, for better or for worse. Decisions on water levels, fishing, and land use are made by the proper officials in order to sustain natural resources and the existing ecosystems.[134] But the good intentions of the surrounding communities can't seem to deter the inevitable effects of climate change on the environment. According to the First National Assessment of the Potential Consequences on Climate

Variability and Change, longer warm seasons may reduce water levels and increase water temperature causing a depletion in zooplankton and phytoplankton, two organisms that "form the very base of aquatic food chains, and are critical to the survival of the many species of fish that live in the Great Lakes."[135]

It's important to remember that what affects wildlife will eventually affect humankind. Climate change is affecting all wildlife, from the elk to the trout, and "will significantly affect almost every aspect of our environment."[136] Decreasing wildlife populations due to climate change can affect not only the sportsman's livelihood but it also can impact local and national industries. According to a report by the Wildlife Management Institute:

- Approximately 42% of that nation's trout and salmon habitat will disappear by the end of the century.
- About 90% of the wetlands in the Prairie Pothole region will vanish contributing to a possible 69% decline in the nation's duck population.
- Game fish numbers will decrease due to the rise in sea level. A significant sea-level increase and water temperature has the potential to destroy coastal salt marshes and sea grass.
- Rising temperatures in the West will prompt elk, deer, and other wildlife to move East.[137]

The climate is always changing. These changes can impact wildlife and their habitats, which is a concern for sportsmen. Changes in the climate are fueling an intense public policy debate. This debate is often driven by two opposing extreme viewpoints. As history has proved, the sensible approach to conservation demonstrated by American sportsmen can have a meaningful impact on public policy in this type of polarized political environment.

---

[66] Reiger, John F. *American Sportsmen and the Origins of Conservation*. Corvallis: Oregon State University Press, 2001. p. 182.
[67] *Ibid.*
[68] Aldrich, Eric. "North America's Wildlife Conservation Model." *Orion: The Hunter's Institute*. <http://www.huntright.org/heritage/AldrichConservationModel.aspx/>.
[69] *Ibid.*
[70] *Ibid.*
[71] *Ibid.*
[72] Mahoney, Shane. "The Seven Sisters: Pillars of the North American Wildlife Conservation Model." *The Bugle*. Sept/Oct. 2004.
[73] *Ibid.*
[74] Reiger *supra* n.66 at 106.
[75] Mahoney, Shane. "Triumph for Man and Nature: The American Wilderness and John Muir Part 1." *The Bugle*. May/June 2005.
[76] Mahoney, Shane. "Triumph for Man and Nature: The American Wilderness and John Muir Part 2." *The Bugle*. Nov/Dec 2005.
[77] Corbis. John Muir's Yosemite. Photograph. "John Muir's Yosemite." *Smithsonian Magazine* By Tory Perrottet. (July 2008). *Smithsonian*. 15 Aug. 2008. Smithsonian. <http://www.smithsonianmag.com/people-places/yosemite.html#>.
[78] Mahoney *supra* n.75.
[79] Mahoney *supra* n.76.
[80] *Ibid.*
[81] *Ibid.*

[82] *Ibid.*

[83] Larson, Christina. "The Emerging Environmental Majority." *Washington Monthly*. May 2006. <http://www.washingtonmonthly.com/features/2006/0605.larson.html>.

[84] Reiger, George. "Our Troubled Tradition: Could the Present Anti-Hunting Movement Date Back Not to Bambi But to the Manicured Suburban Lawn?" *Field and Stream*. Feb 1994.

[85] "Kodiak National Wildlife Refuge." *U.S. Fish & Wildlife Service*. <http://www.fws.gov/refuges/profiles/index.cfm?id=74530>.

[86] Van Daele, Larry. "Kodiak Brown Bear Fact Sheet." *Alaska Department of Fish & Game Wildlife Conservation*. <http://www.wildlife.alaska.gov/index.cfm?adfg=bears.trivia>.

[87] *Ibid.*

[88] Stienstra, Tom. "Enviros and hook-n-bullet set form unlikely alliance." *San Francisco Chronicle*. 01 May 2008. <http://www.sfgate.com/cgi-bin/article.cgi?f=/c/a/2008/05/01/SPQ810D7C3.DTL>.

[89] Schwedler, Jon, and Carl Pope. "America's Wild Legacy: Building Resilient Habitats." *Sierra Sportsmen*. Sierra Club. 29 May 2008. <http://www.sierraclub.org/wildlegacy/resilienthabitat/>.

[90] Herring, Hal. "Today's Sportsmen and Sportswomen Are A Powerful Force for Conservation." *The Nature Conservancy*. 2008. <http://www.nature.org/magazine/autumn2006/features/art18601.html>.

[91] Sather, Nancy and Robert Dana. "Tallgrass Aspen Parkland." *Minnesota Department of Natural Resources*. 29 May 2008. <http://www.dnr.state.mn.us/volunteer/janfeb99/parkland.html>.

[92] Herring *supra* n.90.

[93] Larson *supra* n.83.

[94] "A Guide to the Laws and Treaties of the United States for Protecting Migratory Birds." *U.S. Fish & Wildlife Service*. 21 May 2002. <http://www.fws.gov/migratorybirds/intrnltr/treatlaw.html#lean>.

[95] Verhey, David M. "General Provisions; Revised List of Migratory Birds." *U.S. Environmental Protection Agency*. Aug 2006. <http://www.epa.gov/fedrgstr/EPA-SPECIES/2006/August/Day-24/e7001.htm>.

[96] Herring *supra* n.90.

⁹⁷ "The Federal Duck Stamp Program." *U.S. Fish & Wildlife Service*. 23 May 2008. <http://www.fws.gov/duckstamps/Info/Stamps/stampinfo.htm>.

⁹⁸ "Division of Realty: Significant Land Acquisition Accomplishments in Fiscal Year 2005." *U.S. Fish & Wildlife Service*. 2005. <http://www.fws.gov/realty/2005accomplishments.html>.

⁹⁹ Overstreet, James. *Ducks Explode From A Pothole*. Photograph. 2007. "Four Called-In Birds." By Mike Suchan. *ESPN Outdoors*. 17 Dec. 2007. <http://sports.espn.go.com/outdoors/general/news/story?id=3155320>.

¹⁰⁰ *U.S. Fish & Wildlife Service, supra* n.98.

¹⁰¹ "Small Wetlands Program: National Wildlife Refuge System." *U.S. Fish & Wildlife Service*. 03 Jun 2008. <http://www.fws.gov/refuges/smallwetlands/FWN.html>.

¹⁰² Satrom, Joseph. "Wetland Loan Act Reauthorization." *FDCH Congressional Testimony*. 07 May 2008. <http://search.ebscohost.com/login.aspx?direct=true&db=ulh&AN=32Y1238469260&site=ehost-live>.

¹⁰³ "Delta Waterfowl Supports Proposal To Raise Price of Federal Duck Stamp: Congress Also Urged to Pass Emergency Wetlands Loan Act." *Delta Waterfowl*. 20 Feb 2008. <http://www.deltawaterfowl.org/pr/2008/080220_duckstamp.php>

¹⁰⁴ "New Report Documents Dramatic Success of Sportsmen-Supported Conservation Tax Incentive Programs." *Theodore Roosevelt Conservation Partnership*. 20 Nov 2006. <http://www.trcp.org/pr_easementsreport.aspx>.

¹⁰⁵ Coates, Peter. "Trans-Alaska Pipeline." *Encyclopedia of World Environmental History: O-Z*. By Shepard Krech, John Robert McNeill, Carolyn Merchant. Published by Routledge, 2003. Page 1218.

¹⁰⁶ *Ibid*.

¹⁰⁷ Coile, Zachary. "The Last Refuge: Caribou Migration, Drilling Plan Symbolic of Battle Between Oil and Environment." *San Francisco Chronicle*. 28 Aug. 2005.

¹⁰⁸ "Trans-Alaska Pipeline System (TAPS) Turns 30." *In The Pipe* 1:3. Dec 2007. <http://www.enewsbuilder.net/inthepipe/e_article000979438.cfm>.

¹⁰⁹ *Ibid*.

[110] Valkenburg, Patrick. "Caribou." *Alaska Department of Fish & Game.* 1999. <http://www.adfg.state.ak.us/pubs/notebook/biggame/caribou.php>.
[111] "Trans Alaska Pipeline System (TAPS) Turns 30, " *supra* n.108.
[112] Arrigo, Mike and Pete Burak, Bradford Coyle. "Environmental Effects of the Alaska Pipeline." *University of Michigan.* <http://sitemaker.umich.edu/section003_group001/home>.
[113] Benson, Lorna. "Hunters and Environmentalists Rally for Ducks and Their Habitat." *Minnesota Public Radio.* April 1, 2005. <http://news.minnesota.publicradio.org/features/2005/03/31_bensonl_noducks/>.
[114] *Ibid.*
[115] "Conservation Easements." *Land Trust Alliance.* <http://www.lta.org/faq/#ce_head>.
[116] "New Report Documents Dramatic Success of Sportsmen-Supported Conservation Tax Incentive Programs." *Theodore Roosevelt Conservation Partnership.* 30 Nov 2008. <http://www.trcp.org/pr_easementsreport.aspx>.
[117] Satrom, Joseph. "Wetland Loan Act Reauthorization." *FDCH Congressional Testimony.* 07 May 2008. <http://search.ebscohost.com/login.aspx?direct=true&db=ulh&AN=32Y1238469260&site=ehost-live>.
[118] *Delta Waterfowl, supra* n.103.
[119] Satrom, *supra* n.102.
[120] Herring *supra* n.90.
[121] Meyer, Kevin A. and Daniel J. Schill. "Summary of 15 Years of IDFG Dingell-Johnson Research, 1988-2003." *Idaho Department of Fish and Game.* Nov 2005. <https://research.idfg.idaho.gov/Fisheries%20Research%20Reports/05-47%20Schill%20DJ%20research%20summary%201988-2003.pdf>.
[122] "What's Happening with the Conservation and Reinvestment Act (CARA)?" *North Carolina Species and Conservation: Conservation News.* <http://www.ncwildlife.org/pg07_WildlifeSpeciesCon/pg7d1.htm>.
[123] DeWeese, Tom. "Return of the CARA Monster." *Enter Stage Right: Politics, Culture, Economics.* 3 May 2004. <http://www.enterstageright.com/archive/articles/0504/0504cara.htm>.

124 *North Carolina Species and Conservation: Conservation News*, supra n.122.
125 Brooke, Rachel and Naomi Edelson, Dave Chadwick, Rachel Brittin, Sean Robertson, Genevieve LaRouche, and Chris Burkett. "State Wildlife Grants Five-Year Accomplishment Report: Cost-Effective Conservation to Prevent Wildlife From Becoming Endangered." *Association of Fish & Wildlife Agencies and the U.S. Fish & Wildlife Service.* <http://www.teaming.com/pdf/swg_report.pdf>.
126 "Farm Bill Makes Hay." Outdoor News Bulletin. *Wildlife Management Institute.* 2008. <http://www.wildlifemanagementinstitute.org/index.php?option=com_content&view=article&id=259:farm-bill&catid=34:ONB%20Articles&Itemid=54>.
127 "Conservation Programs Win with Passage of Farm Bill: Congressional Sportsmen's Caucus Preserves Funding." *Congressional Sportsmen's Foundation* 15 May 2008 Press Release. <http://www.sportsmenslink.org/pdf/CSF_FarmBill-5-15-08.pdf>.
128 LaFramboise, Nathan. "The Cormorant Conflict." *Animal Legal & Historical Center.* Michigan State University College of Law. 2006. <http://www.animallaw.info/articles/dduscormorantconflict.htm>.
129 "Federal Lawsuit Filed Fights for Birds." *Parks & Recreation.* April 2004. <http://search.ebscohost.com/login.aspx?direct=true&db=aph&AN=12860591&site=ehost-live>.
130 Collier, B. and D.V. Weseloh. "The Rise of the Double-crested Cormorant on the Great Lakes: Winning the War Against Contaminants." *Canadian Wildlife Service and Long Point Bird Observatory.* 10 Oct 2005. <http://www.on.ec.gc.ca/wildlife/factsheets/fs_cormorants-e.html>.
131 *Double-Crested Cormorants are making a comeback in the Great Lakes region.* Photograph. *Geography Unit 15-16: Great Lakes.* Ed. Irwin D'Souza, et al. 9 Mar. 2006 20 Aug. 2008. <http://geo.atspace.com/UrbanExpansion>.
132 Collier and Weseloh, *supra* n.130.
133 LaFramboise, *supra* n.128.
134 Fisk, Aaron and Hugh MacIsaac. "Cormorant Cull Needed." *The Windsor Star.* 08 Apr 2008. <http://www.canada.com/windsorstar/news/editorial/story.html?id=a4913bb6-2598-423b-bf48-6f5853551981&p=1>.

[135] Glick, Patty and Peter Sousounis, Ph.D. "The Potential Impacts of Global Warming on the Great Lakes." *Critical Findings for the Great Lakes Region from the First National Assessment of the Potential Consequences of Climate Variability and Change.* 2000. <http://www.climatehotmap.org/impacts/greatlakes.html>.
[136] Hebert, Josef H. "Hunters Worry About Global Warming." *The Associated Press.* 10 Apr 2008. <http://www.sfgate.com/cgi-bin/article.cgi?f=/n/a/2008/04/10/national/w001644D70.DTL>.
[137] *ibid.*

What You Should Know About Climate Change

Sportsmen and environmentalists aren't the only ones concerned about the perceived impacts of climate change. Globally, people are responding to public calls for action. Climate change can alter ecosystems as large as the Sahara or as small as your backyard. In addition to its potential impact on the environment and the wildlife in it, climate change and public policy proposals to address it will also affect the economy and society. Despite widespread media attention, many people don't know what climate change is; without understanding the issue, how can we develop strategies to address it?

Many nationwide surveys conducted by leading news stations and research centers in recent years show an increase in environmental awareness among the general public. However, a large percentage of Americans remain skeptical and confused about climate change.

- 38% of survey participants think climate change is a theory that has yet to be proven.[138]
- 47% understand climate change "somewhat well" compared to 32% who feel they know it "very well."[139]
- 34% believe climate change is a serious problem and immediate action is necessary.[140]
- 63% feel the U.S. is in as much danger from the threat of climate change as it is to terrorists.[141]
- 33% of Americans surveyed feel climate change is the biggest global problem in 2007; 16% in 2006.[142]

- 49% think climate change is seriously impacting our world, compared to 35% in 2001.[143]
- 70% are willing to spend $500 or less each year on higher energy prices in order to address climate change.[144]
- 35% are unwilling to spend any money on higher energy prices to address climate change.[145]

The issue isn't that the climate is changing; climate has naturally transformed over thousands of years and will continue to do so. The question that is being debated today is whether man's actions are accelerating the speed at which changes to the climate cycle are occurring. Climate change refers to the consistent pattern of weather in a given region over an elongated period of time. It's often referred to as, but should not be confused with, global warming. Global warming relates to a more widespread result of climate change. We associate certain areas (like the Amazon River Basin, for example) with particular climate patterns (high temperatures, heavy precipitation). Climate change occurs when these patterns shift, altering one or more of these weather-related properties.

Climate change occurs naturally, like the progression of the ice ages, and may be caused by differences in the Sun's intensity, a shift in the Earth's orbit, or even a variation in the oceans' currents.[146] External influences also have an impact on the planet. Urbanization and deforestation are some common examples of human that have an ecological impact. In a poll conducted by STATS, a nonpartisan research group, 84 percent of scientists speculate that warming in recent years is due, in part, to human activity.[147] It is difficult to say whether one factor or the other is the primary cause for climate change. However, if there are opportunities for us sportsmen to reduce our environmental footprint while potentially contributing to a solution to accelerated climate change, then we should assume a leadership position.

The retention of greenhouse gases (GHGs) in the atmosphere is, in part, a cause of climate change. Necessary to human survival, the greenhouse effect refers to the trapping and building-up of heat in the atmosphere (troposphere). Heat from the sun comes down to earth and is either absorbed into the atmosphere and reflects back to earth or returns to space in the form of infrared waves. Some of the heat that leaves the earth is trapped by atmospheric gases (water vapor and carbon dioxide, for example) and warms our planet. Much like gardeners use greenhouses to trap heat and protect their plants, the greenhouse effect keeps the earth warm and helps to regulate seasonal changes. The theory of global warming takes the greenhouse effect one step further. Instead of a warm/cool balance, the greenhouse effect may escalate the warming trend as more and more heat is captured. Such an increase could be partly responsible for the melting of glaciers, irregularity in seasons, and heavier precipitation in some areas.

Greenhouse gases are important to understanding climate change because they soak up infrared radiation in the atmosphere contributing to the warming trend. Concentration levels of GHGs are a major concern of environmentalists and scientists today, and a prime focus of environmental legislation. New plans call for the reduction in GHG emissions by major industries in efforts to "go green" and thwart the potentially disastrous effects of climate change. While only 5.53% of all greenhouse gas emissions come from man, which are called "anthropogenic interference," it is speculated that manmade GHGs may be tipping the balance maintained by naturally occurring greenhouse gases, and may accelerate the natural cycle of climate change.[148]

Four greenhouse gases are among the dominant and most widely regulated by governments in climate change mitigation efforts. The first, and most common, is carbon dioxide (CO_2). Since the Industrial Revolution, the amount of atmospheric carbon dioxide has risen more than 30 percent.[149] Carbon dioxide levels may be influenced by a variety of natural and human influences: population influx, economic growth, energy use, seasonal changes in temperature, and even technological changes.[150] The U.S. Environmental Protection Agency estimates that the annual growth rate of CO_2 emissions is approximately 1.1 percent, and made up 84.8 percent of U.S. GHG emissions in 2006.[151]

The Intergovernmental Panel on Climate Change (IPCC) developed a system in which to define and compare the potency of greenhouse gases, called Global Warming Potential (GWP). The GWP system uses carbon dioxide as a reference gas, a point from which to measure the strength of other gases because it has the lowest potency of all the greenhouse gases. The GWP of a gas is measured as the radiative force a gas has over an extended period of time (in this case, 100 years) that occurs from emissions of a unit mass of gas compared to that of a reference gas.[152] Carbon dioxide has a GWP of 1.

The second greenhouse gas, methane (CH_4) is 20 times more effective in trapping heat than carbon dioxide and has a GWP of 23.[153] Unlike carbon dioxide, CH_4 numbers have risen 148 percent since the mid-1700s.[154] Methane accounts for approximately nine percent of greenhouse gas emissions and is produced both naturally and by humans.[155] Anthropogenic sources can be found in livestock management, rice cultivation and production, fossil fuel extraction, and waste treatment facilities. Naturally, CH_4 can be found abundantly in wetland areas where there is little to no oxygen. These areas comprise about 80 percent of natural CH_4 emissions. Other natural sources include termites, vegetation, oceans, and methanogens, small microorganisms that digest carbon dioxide and release methane into the atmosphere.[156]

Landfills are considered to be the largest source of human-made methane emissions. This is partly attributed to food waste that decomposes; food waste makes up approximately 12 percent of landfill garbage. Scientists suggest that by shopping smarter (planning out grocery lists, for example) and portioning our food we can cut down on our waste and thus, our contribution to methane emissions.[157] There is also existing technology to extract this gas from landfills and use it to generate electricity instead of venting it into the atmosphere. This electricity can displace other sources of electrical generation. Increasing the number of landfills using this technology to capture methane is an emission reduction strategy that can be employed today.

Nitrous oxide (N_2O) is another powerful greenhouse gas. More effective than carbon dioxide, N_2O has a GWP of 296,[158] and it is approximately 300 times more powerful than CO_2.[159] Concentrations of nitrous oxide in the atmosphere have risen more than 15 percent since the end of the Industrial Revolution, but between 1990 and 2006, levels decreased by four percent.[160]

Currently, N_2O accounts for about 5 percent of total greenhouse gas emissions.[161] About 72 percent of this comes from agricultural fertilizers and soils rich in nitrogen, with the rest attributed to waste management fields, cattle and cattle feed production, and biomass burning.[162] Newer pollution-control technologies are helping curb the onset of increasing nitrous oxide concentrations since the 1990s but emissions are still on the rise. According to the IPCC Special Report on Emissions Scenarios, the future of N_2O emissions rests on the size, structure, and placement of global populations and the direction of agricultural production.[163] This means that developers, urban planners, and vehicle designers may need to consider their emissions levels and how those emissions may affect the environment.

In 2000, collaboration between shipping giant, FedEx, and the Environmental Defense Fund (EDF) brought about a new trend in how companies ship and deliver their products. FedEx wanted a way to reduce their emissions and promote a positive outlook on the environment. Their solution was to use hybrid delivery trucks that ran on diesel and electric. Based on 1999 records, the new vehicles emit 65 percent less nitrous oxide into the atmosphere and have an increase in fuel efficiency of over 50 percent. One hundred and seventy hybrid FedEx trucks were expected to rule the road by the end of 2008.[164]

Using a new system called regenerative breaking, a process that recaptures the heat from braking rather than losing it, these delivery trucks are more fuel efficient and are likely to require less maintenance than other non-alternative fuel vehicles. The partnership has sparked interest among other companies who want to exhibit a leadership position on reducing greenhouse gas emissions. Coca-Cola, AT&T, Verizon, and Florida Power & Light have purchased, or are making plans to purchase, hybrid vehicles. Even FedEx's competitor UPS has adopted hybrid delivery trucks![165] By working cooperatively to reduce their emissions, FedEx and the EDF became pioneers at finding cost-effective ways to reduce environmental impact. While some greenhouse gases can be reduced through more fuel-efficient, eco-friendly methods, other GHGs are harder to address.

Fluorocarbons make up the last main group of greenhouse gases. Despite their relatively low concentrations, they may be some of the most potent gases in the atmosphere. Also called F-Gases, these contain other elements such as hydrogen, bromine, or chlorine, and are commonly used in manufacturing and commercial industries. Together, they make up approximately two percent of greenhouse gas emissions.[166]

Chlorofluorocarbons (CFCs), used in refrigeration and packaging, are considered to be dangerous to the ozone layer.[167] Rather than disintegrate into the lower atmosphere, CFCs drift upward and eat away at the ozone layer. Because of their threat to the ozone and the environment, other fluorocarbons were introduced in hopes of offsetting the negative effects. Hydroflurocarbons (HFCs) and perfluorocarbons (PFCs), for example, are used in manufacturing and commercial needs and are extremely powerful greenhouse gases.[168] Most potent, according to the IPCC, is sulfurhexafluoride (SF_6). This chemical can live in the atmosphere about 3,000 years and has a GWP over 22,000.[169]

Studies show that greenhouse gas emissions have steadily risen since the Industrial Revolution and continue to do so, but it is rather difficult to gauge how much of those emissions are from human activity. From 1990 to 2006 total U.S. GHG emissions have climbed approximately 15 percent, with a decrease of 1.1 percent between 2005 and 2006. The drop can be attributed to weather, fuel prices, and the increased use of renewable energy sources and natural gas.[170]

Research has shown our climate has been fairly stable over the last 2,000 years, with three minor departures: the Medieval Climate Anomaly, the Little Ice Age, and the Industrial Era. The Medieval Climate Anomaly was a period of warmer, drier weather that occurred between 900 and 1300 AD in Europe, Asia, and the North America. Between the 16th and 19th centuries, the Little Ice Age brought cooler temperatures to various regions. Steady temperature increases have been noted in the past 100 years. Called the Industrial Age, some scientists believe that this warmer weather coincides with increased industrial activities.[171] Others, like Dr. Syun-Ichi Akasofu, Professor of Physics, Emeritus at the University of Alaska Fairbanks, believe this warming is primarily attributed to the fact that the Earth is still coming out of the Little Ice Age.[172]

Other records have yielded rather interesting results about the stability of our planet's weather patterns. The United Kingdom's national weather service, MetOffice, and a group of British academics discovered Royal Navy logbooks dating back to the 17th Century that may be helpful in understanding, and maybe better predicting, climate changes. As far back as the 1600s, ships did not have the technology to record temperatures and atmospheric changes but captains used consistent language to describe the weather changes. From the details provided in the logs, scientists are working to construct a picture of Europe's past weather conditions.[173]

The logbooks have also prompted questions about the sources of climate change. The Little Ice Age between the 16th and 19th century, in particular, is of special interest to geographer, Dr. Dennis Wheeler of Sunderland University in the United Kingdom. Between the 1680s and 1690s a surge of summer storms passed through Europe that many other scientists believe is related to global warming. However, the logbooks have revealed that these storms occurred during the coldest period of the Little Ice Age. There was also a period of warming during 1730 that may point to natural, not man-made, sources of climate change.[174]

In the Arctic, average temperatures have increased dramatically causing glaciers and ice sheets to melt. The U.S. Center for Atmospheric Research estimates that the Arctic could possibly be without ice by the year 2040.[175] Globally, the sea level has risen between four to eight inches in the last century and could increase up to 23 inches by 2100. Greenland holds approximately ten percent of the world's ice mass and, if it melts, could increase the sea level by 21 feet.[176] In 2007, levels of sea ice were at the lowest ever recorded with an approximate 39 percent decline from long-term averages in the last 20 years. Moreover, the levels from 2002-2007 indicate a consistent loss of sea ice exceeding any other recorded levels.[177] These alterations are not only affecting the land but also the wildlife that lives in the region.

Looking at the change in habitat for the polar bear can exemplify the possible ripple effects climate change could likely have on the American sportsman. Immediately following its admittance onto the Endangered Species list, the U.S. government banned all polar bear hunting. Taking the ruling one step further, the legislation also prohibits the importation of polar bear prize hides into the U.S. This new law may have serious repercussions for sport hunters.

Currently, Canada does not hold a ban on polar bear hunting but limits the season to a two-month period distributing only 40 permits a year.[178] Sport hunters can pay thousands of dollars just for the chance to hunt for polar bear in the Canadian wilderness. Approximately 200 hunters a year get that opportunity and even less (an estimated one-half) get their shot. American hunters are already restricted as to what they can hunt within our own borders and, with the ban on prize imports, even the small number of hunters likely to have a successful hunt aren't able to bring home their trophy.[179] With the potential for more species to fall victim to climate change, there is the likelihood of tighter restrictions and regulations placed on sportsmen and their game through similar bans.

Many American sportsmen in an uproar over the ban are encouraging legislators to rethink the listing—and the ban. In early 2008, leaders of the Congressional Sportsmen's Foundation, members of American Wildlife Conservation Partnership (AWCP), and members from twenty national sportsmen's organizations signed a petition to appeal the ban.[180] The letter outlines economic contributions from sportsmen to research groups and other areas of conservation. The number totals nearly $1 million since 1994 for polar bear research and conservation initiatives. In addition, each import permit provides about $1,000 to polar bear research in the U.S. and Russia.[181] Senator Jim Inhofe of Oklahoma – a member of the Congressional Sportsmen's Caucus – disagrees with the ESA's listing claiming that it is more likely to prove unhelpful to the polar bear and local native populations that rely on the hunts for annual income.[182] Further information included in the letter states:

> [A] ban would not decrease polar bear mortality from hunting. The native holders of tags not used by the U.S. hunters would simply use them to harvest polar bears for subsistence . . . . [T]he annual "quota" the Canadian provincial governments create determines the number of polar bears harvested each year . . . . [T]he U.S. and Canadian governments repeatedly have determined that properly regulated subsis-

tence and sport hunting are not a threat to the polar bear populations.[183]

While sportsmen may not be a real threat to polar bears, the shift in our planet's climate and the weather patterns created as a result pose a risk to many species. Anthropologist Polly Wheeler, of the U.S. Fish and Wildlife Service of Alaska, spoke with hunters and anglers who live and visit the Arctic region. Sportsmen delivered some very troubling news about the wildlife, in particular the caribou herds of the region. Hunters are noting a decline in the caribou population, a loss partly due to higher mortality rates among calves and vulnerability throughout their lives.[184]

In 1998, there was an estimated 95 percent decrease in the Peary caribou herd numbers since the early 1960s.[185] Climate change has started to affect food availability, making it difficult for pregnant female caribou and calves to get adequate nutrition. By the time the caribou comes to feed, plant life has already reached its peak nutritional value as the plants respond to temperatures, not daylight.[186] Associate Professor of Biology at Penn State Eric Post puts it simply:

> Think of it like this . . . . You've been out on the town with friends, and on the way home you want to stop off for a bite to eat, but the restaurant you've always gone to has closed early. So you try for one around the corner . . . it too is closed. For herbivores, the fact that there are several "restaurants"—their

food patches—dispersed across the landscape isn't useful if they all begin closing at the same time in addition to closing earlier in the season.[187]

Without good, consistent food sources, caribou are likely to become more vulnerable to attacks from wolves and other predators. If climate change continues at this rate, it's possible that the Arctic Peary caribou herd could become extinct and several other herds could be severely reduced in number.

Anglers are finding that the quality and health of salmon is declining as well. Warmer water temperatures have made the streams and rivers where salmon live virtually uninhabitable, as salmon thrive off cold fresh water.[188] In Tanana, Alaska, for example, anglers are noticing a disease in salmon that may be related to climate change. As the water temperature increases, parasites and bacteria can flourish and thus, have a better chance of survival. A parasite called *Ichthyophonus hoferi* has infected the salmon causing, what some call, the "white spot disease," or Ich. Ich appears as tiny white spots on the fish's organs and causes a stench similar to that of rotting fruit.[189] It's been known to kill the fish it infects and can also affect salmon reproduction.[190] This is yet another example of how climate change is affecting the livelihood of sportsmen; anglers are tossing out over 1/4 of what they catch as a result of the disease.[191]

Further south, in Oregon and California, the Pacific Fishery Management Council has agreed to ban Atlantic salmon fishing due to the virtual disappearance of the species. In April 2008, Governor Arnold Schwarzenegger of California declared a state of emergency for the fishing community. Salmon production has declined to about 65,000 from 800,000 in just six years. Both commercial and recreational anglers are concerned for the sport and the species. What troubles many sportsmen is the lack of understanding of the reasons for the decline; no one is sure why salmon numbers have fallen. Biologists speculate the possibilities of damaged habitat, water pollution, and water diversion. Just as the Ich disease has compromised the Arctic salmon it's possible that bacteria and parasites, which thrive in warm water, could be hurting their counterparts in the Atlantic.

The ban is putting a strain on many anglers and causing a strain on others who lose their livelihoods. In California, anglers stand to lose an estimated $20.7 million and up to 80 percent of their annual income if the ban holds. Oregon's losses are smaller, at an estimated $9 million. But anglers are following the true code of the sportsman: "[T]o most anglers, the situation isn't about money anymore. It's about survival of a species."[192]

The potential hazards posed by climate change include more than warmer waters and melting glaciers. Globally, the sea level has risen approximately 5-10 inches in the last century.[193] Rainfall has increased in the last 100 years with exception in the tropics. Areas familiar to heavy precipitation are becoming wetter while it's becoming drier in arid regions.[194]

Although there is no specific evidence to suggest that climate change worsens hurricanes and tropical storms, they are estimated to become "wetter and fiercer" during the annual U.S. hurricane seasons from June to November.[195] These alterations affect the wildlife and those who live in the region but they also impact sportsmen. Climate change could destroy those landscapes that sportsmen have come to love. It could also threaten the quality and number of wildlife, making it difficult for hunters and anglers to enjoy their sport. With no animals to hunt there is no hunting.

Anglers may not think of melting glaciers while struggling to pull in a large mouth bass while sitting on a boat in the hot Florida sun, but perhaps they should be. The reduction of sea ice can have tremendous effects on how these men and women spend their time and make a living. Rising sea levels and warmer waters are bound to have a troubling effect on how marine ecosystems function. While the effects may be somewhat subtle at present, they won't remain that way for long. According to Dr. Luiz Barbieri of the Marine Fisheries Research Section of the Florida Fish and Wildlife Conservation Commission, saltwater marshes will move upland, disrupting nursing and feeding areas; zooplankton and other vital microorganisms will reduce in number; and disease will increase among marine species.[196] As weather conditions become less hospitable and conducive for survival, many marine species could die out. Anglers everywhere are seeing first-hand how climate change is having an effect on various species of fish and are noticing how some are adapting to their changing environments, while others risk extinction.

While the West Coast of the United States has seen dwindling numbers of salmon, the East Coast has charted warmer water temperatures and their effect on the lobster population. Off the coast of Long Island Sound, the homarus americanus lobster is dying out. Since 1998 there has been an approximate 60-70 percent decline in lobster numbers. Some scientists posit warmer waters as a possible cause for the decrease.[197] Local anglers have recorded annual drops from over 12 million pounds in the early 1990s to no more than three million pounds in recent years. They too, like those on the West Coast, are losing millions of dollars, their livelihoods, and their sport.[198]

Take the case of a Connecticut lobsterman who was close to retiring when the decline began. He and his wife sold their house, car and lobster boat and relocated to Naples, Florida. In an interview with the Boston Globe he said: "when they [the lobsters] disappeared, we lost the business, we lost everything. I can't tell you how much I miss it. Not being out on the water every day. You know, the sun, the wind. It was a great life."[199]

These are some of the changes that scientists studying climate change have been predicting; the alteration of habitat leading to the decline of a species can ultimately lead to a rise or fall of another. When species integral to an ecology are wiped out, it is likely that others will follow. These same changes are also linked to the habitats of other terrestrial species.

On land, many animal species are disappearing as increased susceptibility to wildfires and disease destroy their food supply. Scientists estimate that in the American West, trees and shrubs are likely to overtake the sagebrush regions that big game animals depend on for survival and protection. Just as diseases thrive in warm water, bacteria also flourish in warmer land temperatures. Sportsmen may find their hunting seasons limited due to dwindling wildlife numbers, or the quality of their game compromised due to lack of nutrition and increased disease. Some researchers predict that the elk and mule deer may disappear entirely as they migrate to find cooler climates to fight disease and find more abundant food supplies.[200] Some say that warmer, drier climates can be very damaging to these elk and deer species. Citizens are so concerned about their hoofed friends that they provide water-trapping devices to help the animals survive since the seasonal weather is no longer conducive to the species' survival.[201]

It is possible that more and more wildlife species will have to rely on human intervention to exist if climate patterns become more unstable. Even with lower GHG emissions, climate changes will still occur; hurricanes and tornadoes will still happen, summer months will continue to be hot, regions near the Equator will still receive heavy precipitation. Debate is ongoing as to whether changes to the climate will be abrupt or more gradual. As the name suggests, abrupt climate change refers to sudden shifts that are capable of producing large amounts of damage in a short time frame. Its cause is unclear therefore it's difficult to predict these potentially severe changes. What scientists do know, however, is that once abrupt climate change is triggered, human beings and all living organisms may have trouble adapting.

A mix of factors can contribute to such an unexpected shift. According to the IPCC's Climate Change 2007 report "changes in weather patterns can result from abrupt changes that might occur spontaneously due to interactions in the atmosphere-ice-ocean system, or from the crossing of a threshold from slow external forcing."[202] The forces behind it can include changes in the Earth's orbit, melting ice sheets, or a shift in ocean currents.

We may not be able to control how climate change affects the weather, but we certainly can control how we react to it. There are sensible, practical steps we can take to counteract the potential negative effects for the benefit of the economy, environment, public health, and international trade.

Sportsmen may be perceived as unlikely environmentalists, but they know more than anyone the kind of changes climate change could bring. Sportsmen have seen climate change affect landscapes, wildlife, and their livelihoods. Hunters and anglers see, with first-hand experience, what is happening to the wildlife and ecosystems of the places we and our loved ones have grown to cherish. Their concern is not only for the welfare of their sport but for the health and preservation of our wildlife, lands, and families. By teaming up with politicians and representatives from environmental and community organizations, sportsmen can help create some of the best and most effective policies for the upcoming decades.

---

[138] *CNN/Opinion Research Corporation.* 21 Jan. 2007. <http://www.pollingreport.com/enviro.htm>.

[139] *Fox New/Opinion Dynamics Poll.* 2 Feb. 2007. <http://www.foxnews.com/projects/pdf/020207_global_warming_web.pdf>.

[140] *NBC News/Wall Street Journal.* 17-20 Jan. 2007. <http://online.wsj.com/public/resources/documents/poll-01-22-07.pdf>.

[141] *Yale Center for Environmental Law & Policy.* 5 Mar 2007. <http://www.eesi.org/briefings/2007/energy_climate/5-4-07_Climate

_polling/Climate%20Polling%20Fact%20Sheet_5.4.07.pdf>.
[142] "Environment Trends." *Washington Post/ABC News Poll.* 20 Apr 2007. <http://www.washingtonpost.com/wp-srv/nation/polls/postpoll_environment_042007.html>.
[143] *CBS News/New York Times.* 26 Apr 2007. <http://www.eesi.org/briefings/2007/energy_climate/5-4-07_Climate_polling/Climate%20Polling%20Fact%20Sheet_5.4.07.pdf>.
[144] *Institute for Energy Research.* April 2008. <http://www.instituteforenergyresearch.org/climate-change/>
[145] *Ibid.*
[143] "Climate Change: Basic Information." *U.S. Environmental Protection Agency.* 01 Apr 2008. <http://www.epa.gov/climatechange/basicinfo.html>.
[144] Lichter, Robert S. "Climate Scientists Agree on Warming, Disagree on Dangers, and Don't Trust the Media's Coverage of Climate Change." STATS. 24 Apr 2008. <http://stats.org/stories/2008/global_warming_survey_apr23_08.html>.
[145] Mullikin, Tom. *Global Solutions: Demanding Total Accountability for Climate Change.* Charlotte: Vox Populi Publishers, LLC, 2007. p 43.
[146] Reay, Dave and Michael Pidwirny (Lead Authors); Jay Gulledge and Sidney Draggan (Topic Editors). "Carbon dioxide." *Encyclopedia of Earth.* Eds. Cutler J. Cleveland. Washington, D.C.: Environmental Information Coalition, National Council for Science and the Environment, 13 Oct 2006. <http://www.eoearth.org/article/Carbon_dioxide>.
[147] "Executive Summary." *Inventory of U.S. Greenhouse Gas Emissions and Sinks: 1990-2006.* U.S. Environmental Protection Agency, 2006. <http://www.epa.gov/climatechange/emissions/downloads/08_ES.pdf>.
[148] *Ibid.*
[149] "Glossary of Climate Change Terms." *U.S. Environmental Protection Agency.* 11 Jan 2008. <http://www.epa.gov/climatechange/glossary.html>.
[150] Reay, Dave. "Methane." *Encyclopedia of Earth.* Eds. Peter Hughes, Cutler J. Cleveland. Washington, D.C.: Environmental Information Coalition, National Council for Science and the Environment, 2006. <http://www.eoearth.org/article/Methane>.

[151] U.S. EPA *supra* n.147.
[152] "Greenhouse Gases, Climate Change, and Energy." *Energy Information Administration*. 02 Apr 2004. <http://www.eia.doe.gov/oiaf/1605/ggccebro/chapter1.html>.
[153] Reay *supra* n.150.
[154] Collins, Karen. "Are You Gonna Eat That? Cut Back on Food Waste." *MSNBC*. 11 Jul 2008. <http://www.msnbc.msn.com/id/25215428/>.
[155] Reay, Dave. "Nitrous Oxide." *Encyclopedia of Earth*. Eds. Peter Hughes, Cutler J. Cleveland. Washington, D.C.: Environmental Information Coalition, National Council for Science and the Environment, 2006. <http://www.eoearth.org/article/Nitrous_oxide>.
[156] U.S. EPA *supra* n.147.
[157] *Ibid.*
[158] *EIA supra* n. 152. <http://www.eia.doe.gov/oiaf/1605/ggccebro/chapter1.html>.
[159] U.S. EPA *supra* n.147.
[160] Nakicenovic, Nebojsa et al. "IPCC Special Report on Emissions Scenarios." *Intergovernmental Panel on Climate Change*. <http://www.grida.no/Climate/ipcc/emission/122.htm>.
[161] "Working with FedEx to Deliver Clean Air." *Environmental Defense Fund*. 8 May 2008. <http://www.edf.org/page.cfm?tagID=2050>.
[162] *Ibid.*
[163] *EIA supra* n. 152.
[164] U.S. EPA *supra* n.149.
[165] *Ibid.*
[166] "Fluorocarbons and sulfurhexafluoride: SF6." *European Fluorocarbons Technical Committee*. <http://www.fluorocarbons.org/en/families/sf6/environmental_aspects.html>
[167] U.S. EPA *supra* n.147.
[168] "Past Climate Change." *U.S. Environmental Protection Agency*. <http://www.epa.gov/climatechange/science/pastcc.html>.
[169] Akasofu, Dr. Syun-Ichi. "The Recovery from the Little Ice Age (A Possible Cause of Global Warming) and The Recent Halting of the Warming (The Multi-decadal Ocilliation)." *Unpublished Paper*. 25 September 2008. <http://people.iarc.uaf.edu/~sakasofu/pdf/recovery_little_ice_age.pdf>

170 Leake, Jonathan. "Captains' Logs Yield Climate Clues." *The Sunday Times*. 3 Aug 2008. <http://www.timesonline.co.uk/tol/news/environment/article4449527.ece>.

171 *Ibid.*

172 "Issues: Global Warming." *NRDC: The Natural Resources Defense Council*. 21 Sep 2007. <http://www.nrdc.org/globalWarming/fcons.asp>.

173 *Ibid.*

174 Wolfe, Shane. "Secretary Kempthorne Announces Decision to Protect." *Wildlife and Conservation News*. The Boone & Crockett Club. 19 May 2008. <http://www.boone-crockett.org/news/news_dc.asp?area=news>.

175 Hebert, Josef F. "Canadians Argue For Polar Bear Hunt." *The Associated Press*. 24 Jun 2008. <http://www.physorg.com/news133495464.html>.

176 Campbell, Colin and Kate Lunau. "The War Over the Polar Bear: Who's Telling the Truth About the Fate of a Canadian Icon?" *MacLeans.ca*. 25 Jan 2008. <http://www.macleans.ca/science/environment/article.jsp?content=20080123_5242_5242&page=1>.

177 "Hunting Groups Oppose Polar Bear 'Endangered' Listing." *Sportsmen's News*. 2 Apr 2008. The Congressional Sportsmen's Foundation. <http://www.sportsmenslink.org/media_room/Press-Releases/Polar-Bear-Listing.html>.

178 "Sporting and Conservation Groups' Opposition to Import Ban on Polar Bear Trophies from Canada." *The Congressional Sportsmen's Caucus*. 2 Apr 2008. <http://www.sportsmenslink.org/media_room/Press-Releases/Polar-Bear-Listing.html>.

179 *Sportsmen's News supra* n. 177.

180 *The Congressional Sportsmen's Caucus supra* n.178.

181 Stone, Marilyn. "Global Warnings: In the Louisiana Bayous, Alaska's Fisheries, and the Halls of the Congress, Three Women Engage with a Warmer World." *BeE Woman Magazine*. Summer 2008. <http://www.beemag.com/articles/sum08/features_globalwarming.shtml>.

182 "Climate Change May Be Driving Arctic Caribou to Extinction, Greenpeace Warns." *Greenpeace*. 19 Oct 1998. <http://archive.greenpeace.org/pressreleases/arctic/1998oct19.html>.

[183] "Climate Change Does Double-whammy To Animals In Seasonal Environments." Penn State. *ScienceDaily*. 26 May 2008. <http://www.sciencedaily.com/releases/2008/05/080521201206.htm>.
[184] *Ibid*.
[185] "Global Warming Threatens Cold Water Fish." *Natural Resources Defense Council*. 21 May 2002. <http://www.nrdc.org/globalWarming/ntrout.asp>.
[186] Weiss, Kenneth R. "Alaska Salmon May Bear Scars of Global Warming." *Los Angeles Times*. 15 Jun 2008. <http://www.latimes.com/news/nationworld/nation/la-na-ichfish15-2008jun15,0,587682.story>.
[187] "Case Study:Alaska." Unnatural Disaster: Global Warming and Our National Parks. *National Parks Conservation Association*. 2007. p.22 <http://www.npca.org/globalwarming/unnatural_disaster_e.pdf>.
[188] Weiss *supra* n.186.
[189] Koopman, John. "Salmon Fishing off California, Oregon banned." *San Francisco Chronicle*. 10 Apr 2008. <http://www.sfgate.com/cgi-bin/article.cgi?f=/c/a/2008/04/10/BAO6103NBB.DTL>.
[190] "Sea Level Changes." *U.S. Environmental Protection Agency*. <http://www.epa.gov/climatechange/science/pastcc.html>.
[191] "Percipitation and Storm Changes." *U.S. Environmental Protection Agency*. <http://www.epa.gov/climatechange/science/pastcc.html>.
[192] "Study: Global Warming Not Worsening Hurricanes." *The Associated Press*. 19 May 2008. <http://news.moneycentral.msn.com/provider/providerarticle.aspx?feed=AP&date=20080519&id=8664109>.
[193] Bipartisan Policy Commission. "Saltwater Fish Fact Sheet." Season's End: Global Warming's Threat to Hunting and Fishing. 2007-2008. <http://www.seasonsend.org/view/web/id/32/topic/Saltwater_fish>.
[194] Faiola, Anthony. "A Knell for Lobsters on Long Island Sound." *Washington Post*. 7 Oct 2007. <http://www.washingtonpost.com/wp-dyn/content/article/2007/10/06/AR2007100601341.html>.
[195] Hladky, Gregory B. "Shell Shocked." 13 Jul 2008. *The Boston Globe*. <http://www.boston.com/news/local/articles/2008/07/13/shell_shocked/>.
[196] Faiola *supra* n.194.

[197] Bipartisan Policy Commission. "Big Game Fact Sheet." Season's End: Global Warming's Threat to Hunting and Fishing. 2007-2008. <http://www.seasonsend.org/view/web/id/28/topic/Big_game>.
[198] Marrero, Diana. "Hunters, Anglers Join Global-Warming Outcry." *The Arizona Republic*. 21 Feb. 2008. <http://www.azcentral.com/arizonarepublic/news/articles/0221enviro-hunters0221.html>.
[199] "Extreme Events." Climate Change: Health and Environmental Effects. Environmental Protection Agency. 21 May 2008. <http://www.epa.gov/climatechange/effects/extreme.html>.

CREATING SOUND SOCIAL POLICY

For generations, sportsmen have labored to match meaningful actions with the facts about important ecological and environmental issues of the day. Matching bold actions with passion to meet real challenges has been the benchmark of success for hunters and anglers across the nation. Continued leadership in our community will require thorough research to understand the complex, global issues confronting our generation and the types of public policy proposals that will be most effective in addressing these issues.

In order for a policy to be effective it must be developed out of careful consideration for *all areas involved*. For such an instrument to work there must be specific knowledge about the central issue and how changing it can affect other areas of life.

In 2005, I led a team of scientists, industry representatives and academics on a trip to Antarctica to see firsthand the impact of climate change on that region. We purposely chose a diverse group with diverse opinions to go on this trip. We had one rule – no fistfights. Otherwise, everything else was fair game.

What we saw on that trip left an impression on all of us. We chartered a boat to make the journey to Antarctica. As we crossed Drake's Passage, we saw huge pieces of ice float by that had broken off of glaciers. It is dramatic images like these that have galvanized people to want to take action on climate change.

While there were no fistfights in our group, there were plenty of lively discussions and areas of disagreement. Despite our differences, everyone who made that trip agreed on one key fact – if public policies are going to be effective in addressing climate change, they must be global solutions. All of us can demonstrate leadership through energy efficiencies in our states and communities, but the ultimate mark of success will require global leadership.

Early efforts to craft public policies to deal with climate change recognized the key fact of global leadership. In 1992, the Earth Summit was held in Rio de Janerio. One hundred and seventy-two countries sent representatives to the Earth Summit – a clear demonstration that global participation was needed to successfully tackle pressing environmental issues. While the agreement crafted to address climate change was based on voluntary, not mandatory, efforts to reduce greenhouse gas emissions, 154 countries, including the United States, signed the treaty.

The agreement at the Earth Summit set the stage for the Kyoto Protocol, which is the policy most people associate with climate change. In the five years that passed between the Earth Summit and the Kyoto Protocol, the commitment to a truly global solution had vanished.

In December 1997, the world's leading economies met in Kyoto, Japan, to craft what was billed as an international solution to address climate change. The Kyoto Protocol that resulted led some countries to enter into binding commitments to reduce greenhouse gas emissions. However, the final treaty divided the world up into two camps: developed countries and developing countries.

Developed and industrialized, Annex I, countries formally entered into these commitments, while developing, Non-Annex I, countries committed voluntarily. During the five-year commitment period between 2008-2012, Annex I countries are expected to reduce emissions five percent below 1990 emissions levels (China and India – the world's largest and third largest emitters of greenhouse gases – were Non-Annex I countries and did not agree to reduce their emissions).

By requiring reductions from developed countries, but not developing ones, the Kyoto Protocol wrote out over forty percent of the world's greenhouse gas emissions. This was justified by the parties negotiating the agreement because developed nations were responsible for the largest share of historical and current emissions, these nations had higher per capita emissions, and developing nations needed emissions to grow in order to meet their social and development needs.

So far 180 countries have ratified the Kyoto Protocol.[203] The United States did sign it but failed to ratify for fear of damaging the economy with estimated economic losses at $400 billion and 4.9 million jobs.[204] This fear was based in the fact that not all countries were required to participate.

Because it was not an international agreement, the Kyoto Protocol has become a failed policy. Writing out nearly half of the world's emissions has meant that global emissions have increased, not decreased, since 1997. According to the United Nations Intergovernmental Panel on Climate Change (IPCC), global greenhouse gas emissions have increased 25 percent between 1990 and 2004.[205]

The results for countries that signed the Kyoto Protocol are not that impressive either. "The U.K. and the Principality of Monaco are the only two European countries that, after pledging to reduce emissions (by 12.5 and 8 percent, respectively) by 2012, appear to be on track. In contrast, Austria, which vowed in 2002 to cut emissions over the next 10 years by 13 percent below 1990 levels, is instead pumping out 15 percent more CO2e than it did in 1990."[206]

The United Nations Framework Convention on Climate Change (UNFCCC) found that emissions from the 40 industrialized countries that have reporting obligations under the convention had grown by 2.3 percent from 2000 to 2006.[207]

While emissions are down 5 percent since 1990, the UNFCCC concluded that the 16-year dip was due entirely to the drop in economic activity (factory and power plant shutdowns) in former Eastern bloc countries such as Russia after the 1989 fall of communist governments, which led to a decline of more than two billion metric tons of CO_2e emissions. Those countries' economies have recovered since 2000, leading to an increase in CO_2e emissions of some 258 million metric tons, according to UNFCCC.[208]

At the time Kyoto was being crafted, the public debate was framed in such a way that if you were for the Kyoto Protocol, you were for the environment and if you were against the Kyoto Protocol, you were against the environment. Now, over ten years later, not much has changed (except for increased emissions). This type of polarized and flawed debate has failed to bring any positive outcome.

Today, the emerging public policy of choice to address climate change is the implementation of a cap-and-trade program. A cap-and-trade program is intended to reduce the amount of greenhouse gases emissions and to use a trading market to help participants in the program achieve compliance. Each participant in the program has a certain number of credits equal to their emissions level. Those participants that make greenhouse gas emission reductions can trade or sell to others who are unable to reduce emissions to target levels.

For example, the cap-and-trade legislation introduced by U.S. Senators Joseph Lieberman and John Warner required a 15 percent reduction in emissions by 2020. Permits can be auctioned off or distributed free to existing emitters. Auctioned permits can provide an extra revenue source for public projects or researching alternative energy while free permits can jumpstart a reduction plan.[209]

Once again, the public debate has been framed the same way as it was for the Kyoto Protocol: if you are for cap and trade, you are for the environment and if you are against cap and trade, you are against the environment.

Getting back to the one key fact that we all agreed on during our Antarctica trip, if there is not a global solution emissions will continue to increase because most of the expected growth in emissions will come from developing countries, the same countries left out of the Kyoto Protocol. According to the U.N. Intergovernmental Panel on Climate Change, between 2000 and 2030 two-thirds to three-quarters of the projected increase in global carbon dioxide emissions will occur in developing countries.[210]

In 2007, China passed the United States to become the number one emitter of greenhouse gases globally. China now accounts for over 18% of the world's carbon dioxide emissions, releasing approximately 700 million metric tons more carbon dioxide than the United States last year. The United States is the second biggest emitter, accounting for approximately 17 percent of global greenhouse gas emissions. India, another developing country, was expected to be the third largest emitter by the end of 2008.

These statistics make it clear that a public policy solution that does not involve every nation is not a leadership position. If the United States adopts a cap-and-trade program, while developing countries are not required to make reductions, global emissions will continue to increase. The Lieberman-Warner climate legislation set a goal of a 15 percent reduction (about 900 million metric tons) in U.S. emissions by 2020. At their current rate, increases in Chinese emissions will exceed this reduction in about 16 months. How is that a leadership position?

The reason climate change policy proposals must contain an international component is that companies will relocate overseas to low-cost nations where there is little or no regulation. This relocation fails to accomplish the goal of reducing global greenhouse gas emissions because emissions "migrate" or "leak" to less regulated countries.

Emission migration not only fails to reduce greenhouse gases, it also results in the loss of U.S. jobs. The United States has lost over 5 million manufacturing jobs since 1998, primarily to developing countries like China and

India.[211] Poorly crafted climate change policy will only continue, and perhaps accelerate, that trend.

Another concern for sportsmen and environmentalists who love the great outdoors is that emission migration can also increase other air emissions like sulfur dioxide and mercury. There is little debate about the negative impacts from these emissions. U.S. industries have made significant reductions in emissions like nitrogen oxide (NOx), sulfur dioxide (SOx) and mercury. However, industries in developing nations like China and India are much less efficient and have higher carbon intensities than U.S. industries. Emissions in China are five times worse and in India they are three times worse than in the U.S., meaning not only will greenhouse gas emissions increase, but so will NOx, SOx, and mercury.

For example, for every $1,000,000 of gross domestic product (GDP) in the United States, 540 metric tons of carbon dioxide is emitted. For the same amount of production in China, 2,840 metric tons of carbon dioxide is emitted.[212] According to the World Bank, 20 of the top 30 dirtiest cities are in China and four are in India.

Ralph Nader had this to say about the ineffectiveness of cap and trade programs in reducing greenhouse gas emissions: "Good intentions to limit big polluters in some countries but not others will turn any meaningful cap into Swiss cheese. It can be avoided by relocating existing and new production of various kinds of CO2-emitting industries to jurisdictions with no or virtually no limits."[213]

So how do we craft an effective social policy to address climate change? Once again we can look to the history of the conservation movement and the sensible, pragmatic approach to policy making of the American sportsman.

The idea of sustainable development is getting a lot of discussion today. But sustainable development is very much like the approach American sportsmen have always taken toward conservation. Sustainable development involves approaching climate change and other environmental issues with a concern for economic, social and environmental processes. The goal for sustainable development is to enhance growth in all areas of society while, at the same time, tackling issues like climate change. Such a task requires merging various policy targets to form a type of checks-and-balances system. It is possible for a nation's economy to grow *and* simultaneously decrease greenhouse gas emissions.

Policies centering on sustainable development that promote the wise use of natural resources can prove economically and environmentally sound. Rather than collide, the paths toward economic, social and environmental growth can reinforce and enhance one another. Climate change policies should focus on environmental effectiveness. A bill that is environmentally effective reduces the negative impacts on land and wildlife while maintaining economic growth.[214] Intelligent policy design and implementation are essential in order to sustain a nation's economy *and* its environment. Tossing environmental issues onto existing policies is not likely to have consistent or sustainable results.[215]

One of the biggest obstacles facing climate change policies lies in the incurred cost to the economy and society. For example, the Congressional Budget Office estimates that a federal cap and trade program will cost the United States $1,200,000,000,000.[216] That is $1.2 trillion dollars. Studies by a range of organizations including the Environmental Protection Agency, Energy Information Agency and MIT all conclude that a cap and trade program will increase energy prices and decrease our nation's gross domestic product. Without a global solution, these costs will be borne by American working families while failing to meaningfully reduce global greenhouse gas emissions. In other words, a total failure for American Sportsmen.

Without careful planning, policies may put people out of work or displace populations. Legislators must consider the costs of administering and implementing policies as well as the indirect costs of maintaining them and how they drive newer, cost-effective technologies. Many cap-and-trade proponents see the auctioning of emissions permits as a way to raise revenue to fund research and development into low-carbon technologies. Development of new technologies will be necessary to establish a less-carbon-intensive energy infrastructure.[217] However, many legislators are already eyeing cap and trade revenue for non-energy programs like health care reform. If the revenue generated from a cap-and-trade program is used to fund a wide array of government programs outside of energy, the research into new technology will suffer. Without new technology, ambitious reductions in greenhouse gas emissions will be impossible.

A final factor that must inform the formulation of policies is that new scientific discoveries will change our understanding of the causes of climate change. Some people have declared that the science is "settled." However, that idea is counterintuitive to the nature of scientific discovery. We must make decisions based on the best available information we have at the time, but we must also be able to adjust to account for new information.

For this reason, it is important that policies and regulations be able to accommodate "new" truths arising from the enormous amount of scientific research that is occurring in the area of climate change. As time goes on, scientists will have an even more precise estimation of the rate of climate change and the effects of man's activities on the global climate. While information is continuously changing and evolving, one constant is that policies and regulations must be able to take into account new science and scientific data.

For example, research in the Gubantonggut Desert in China, as well as the Mojave Desert in the United States, indicates that deserts may take up carbon dioxide at the same rate as some temperate forests. There is much research yet to be done in this area, but if the initial findings hold true, then deserts and semi-arid regions of the world may be absorbing 5.2 billion tons of carbon a year. That amount is roughly half the amount of carbon released annually from the burning of all fossil fuels.[218]

This bit of scientific evidence has tremendous implications for future climate change policy. Indeed, this new understanding of the world's deserts as a significant carbon sink suggests that we have not yet begun to scratch the surface of a true understanding of the carbon cycle. It is imperative, then, that public policies be adaptable to changing conditions and new scientific findings.

Considering the challenges that have plagued the development of climate change policy to date, policy makers should consider five key principles as efforts to address this issue move forward. The five key principles in creating workable policies and regulations to address climate change require that they be:

1. Flexible in application;
2. Global in scope;
3. Market-driven in implementation;
4. Firmly anchored in economic reality;
5. Successful in demonstrating tangible environmental benefits.

Even as the policy debate plays out, action can and is being taken by people who are not on the extremes of this issue, but are concerned about taking steps to improve the environment while providing for their families. People debate about reducing emissions by 70 or 80 percent, while failing to acknowledge that few nations have reduced emissions at all. We need to set realistic goals that can be achieved with current technology as we wait for new technology that can take us further to be developed. With current technology there is much that can be done to get us started taking those first steps that are so important in making real, meaningful progress.

Many efforts are helping to reduce emissions and make the world a greener place. Environmentalists aren't the only ones who are concerned about the state of the environment. U.S. corporate leaders are worried about their emissions and how their practices may be affecting the planet.

American industries are working with the Environmental Protection Agency (EPA) to form Climate Leaders, a government-industry partnership concentrating on leaving a clean mark on the environment. Participating companies assess their current greenhouse gas emissions, work with the EPA on creating the most effective strategies to reduce emissions levels, and report their progress annually. As of July 2008, nearly 200 companies have entered the program. Some of the largest companies in America are setting ambitious goals and outlining their development. Manufacturing company, S.C. Johnson, met its initial goal of a 17 percent reduction in GHG emissions from 2000-2005, and is furthering reductions by eight percent before 2010. Other partners include Bank of America, Publix Supermarkets, General Electric Company, Sprint and the Miller Brewing Company.[219]

Climate Leader company Cummins Inc., a corporation that manufactures and distributes fuel systems, power generation systems, and emissions solutions has vowed to reduce emissions by 25 percent between 2005 and 2010.[220] The industry is known for investing in cleaner alternative-fuel technology in engines and developing enviro-friendly solutions in transportation.

The Energy Star program, a labeling system designed by the U.S. Environmental Protection Agency and the U.S. Department of Energy, is gaining in popularity as consumers look for ways to save money and reduce their environmental footprint. The project started in 1992 as a way to help consumers identify products that can reduce emissions and energy bills. Computers and monitors were among the first to be labeled with the Energy Star. Shortly thereafter home appliances, office equipment and heating and cooling systems were included under the system. Now, the Energy Star program has expanded to include industrial buildings and new homes. Energy Star's website records 2007 as its most successful year in energy conservation and emissions reduction. American consumers who purchased the labeled products saved an estimated $16 million on utility bills and prevented nearly 40 billion metric tons of GHG emissions.

Over 14,000 companies across several different industries have become partners of the Energy Star program. These partners either produce goods to meet the Energy Star standards or practice energy-saving methods in their management and production. Companies like Frito-Lay, Bank of America and 3M have signed on as partners in the recent years.[221]

As these examples show, we can start taking action even as the policy debate and scientific research continues. Planning for the future starts now. Whether you are an environmentalist, politician or sportsman, you can make a difference. You can take small steps at home, at work, or while enjoying the outdoors to help make the world a greener place.

---

[203] "Kyoto Protocol." *United Nations Framework Convention on Climate Change.* <http://unfccc.int/kyoto_protocol/items/2830.php>.
[204] West, Larry. "Should the United States Ratify the Kyoto Protocol?" *About.com.* <http://environment.about.com/od/kyotoprotocol/i/kyotoprotocol_2.htm>.

[205] "Trends in Global Greenhouse Gas Emissions." *Netherlands Environmental Assessment Agency.* <http://www.mnp.nl/en/dossiers/Climatechange/TrendGHGemissions1990-2004.html>
[206] Biello, David. "From Bad to Worse: Latest Figures on Global Greenhouse Gas Emissions." *Scientific American* 17 November 2008. <www.sciam.com/article.cfm?id=from-bad-to-worse-with-greenhouse-gas-emissions>
[207] "UNFCCC: Rising industrialized countries emissions underscore urgent need for political action on climate change at Poznan meeting." *United Nations Framework on Climate Change.* 17 November 2008. Press Release. <http://unfccc.int/files/press/news_room/press_releases_and_advisories/application/pdf/081117_ghg_press_release.pdf>.
[208] Biello, David. "From Bad to Worse: Latest Figures on Global Greenhouse Gas Emissions." *Scientific American* 17 November 2008. <www.sciam.com/article.cfm?id=from-bad-to-worse-with-greenhouse-gas-emissions>
[209] Gupta, S., et al. 2007: Policies, Instruments and Co-operative Arguments. In Climate Change 2007: Mitigation, Contribution of Working Group III to the Fourth Assessment Report of the Intergovernmental Panel on Climate Change [B. Metz, O.R. Davidson, P.R. Bosch, R. Dave, L.A. Meyer (eds.)], Cambridge University Press, Cambridge, United Kingdom and New York, NY, USA.
[210] *Ibid.*
[211] *U.S. Bureau of Labor Statistics.* December 2008. <http://data.bls.gov/PDQ/outside.jsp?survey=sm>
[212] *U.S. Energy Information Agency.* December 2008. <http://www.eia.doe.gov/pub/international/iealf/tableh1gco2.xls>.
[213] Nader, Ralph, Toby Heap. "We Need a Global Carbon Tax: The cap-and-trade approach won't stop global warming." *Wall Street Journal* 3 December 2008.
[214] Gupta *supra* n.209.
[215] Sathaye, J., et al. 2007; Sustainable Development and Mitigation. In Climate Change 2007: Mitigation. Contribution of Working Group III to the Fourth Assessment Report of the Intergovernmental Panel on Climate Change [B. Metz, O.R. Davidson, P.R. Bosch, R. Dave, L.A.

Meyer (eds)], Cambridge University Press, Cambridge, United Kingdom and New York, NY, USA.

[216] "S. 2191: America's Climate Security Act of 2007." *Congressional Budget Cost Estimate*. Congressional Budget Office. 10 April 2008. <www.cbo.gov/ftpdocs/91xx/doc9120/s2191.pdf>.

[217] "International Climate Change Programs: Lessons Learned from the European Union's Emissions Trading Scheme and the Kyoto Protocol's Clean Development Mechanism." *United States Government Accountability Office*. GAO-09-151. November 2008. Page 10.

[218] Wohlfahrt, Georg, Lynn F. Fenstermaker, John A. Arnone III. "Large Annual Net Ecosystem CO_2 Uptake of a Mojave Desert Ecosystem." *Global Change Biology* 14 (2008): 1475-1487. Print.

[219] "Climate Leaders: Partners." *U.S. Environmental Protection Agency*. 2 July 2008. <http://www.epa.gov/stateply/partners/index.html>.

[220] *Ibid*.

[221] *Energy Star Website*. <http://www.energystar.gov/index.cfm?c=home.index>.

How to Reduce Your Environmental Footprint

Sportsmen have long been at the forefront of the environmental conservation movement since its inception. In 1887, George Bird Grinnell joined Teddy Roosevelt to found the Boone and Crockett Club, an organization dedicated to the conservation of America's wetlands and wildlife. Grinnell went on to organize the first Audubon Society, and Roosevelt became the first American President to consider the long-term needs for efficient conservation of our national resources, winning the support of fellow hunters and fishermen to bolster his political base. These men knew that the land and wildlife should be revered and protected and that American sportsmen were on the frontline to do something about it. Sportsmen continue to be an integral part of the conservation movement in this country and around the world. By working in cooperation with their communities, local, state and national governments, sportsmen are making positive changes to better our nation and planet everyday.

You don't have to stop enjoying the outdoors or make substantial lifestyle changes to begin to actively reduce your environmental footprint. Joining the conservation movement does not mean you have to give up the activities, foods, products or outdoor lifestyle you love. You can "go green" in a variety of different ways. Simply by purchasing some of the available energy-efficient products available on the market today or by participating in local clean-up projects, you can begin to help make a positive change in our world.

Sportsmen are taking steps now—and have been for hundreds of years—to reduce their environmental impact and subsequently to help protect our land and wildlife for future generations. The time is right to pick up their challenge and continue the fight. Sportsmen have met the challenge for generations to protect ecosystems while enhancing responsible and fair hunting and fishing. We will explore opportunities to take this challenge to the next level and protect our environment for future generations.

Everyday Tips to Reduce Your Environmental Footprint in the Wild

Hunters and anglers rely on untouched, natural areas for outdoor enjoyment. The paradox created by these activities is that the more hunters and fishermen recreate in the great outdoors, the more likely the environment will be altered, and thus reduce the pleasure of the experience. Humankind cannot go into a natural area without leaving a footprint of some type. Therefore, all sportsmen are challenged to leave nature exactly as we found it. This is a worthwhile principle to live by, whether the footprint consists of unsightly trash left behind at a campsite or invisible air pollution.

Many products are now on the market that enable the sportsman to practice environmental stewardship while still feeling the joy of outdoor activities, such as hunting, fishing, boating, hiking and camping. One of the major ways in which a sportsman can reduce his impact on the environment is to think in terms of using manually operated devices when possible and to use rechargeable or solar powered electrical appliances. On a larger and more expensive scale, there are solar panels that can provide clean and free electrical energy to light a hunting lodge or cabin. For the remainder of this chapter, we will review some products and other ideas to help sportsmen reduce their footprint on the outdoors.

Manual Appliances and Hand-Cranked Electric Models

In the "old days" – about five years ago – sportsmen were required to carry kerosene, a white gasoline or propane to power lanterns and cook stoves. If the sportsman used electricity, traditional alkali or rechargeable batteries usually supplied it. Nowadays, a hand-cranked generator, after a minute or two of turning, can power flashlights, lanterns, and electronic equipment for an hour or more. Better still, some appliances, such as blenders and coffee grinders for your camp are non-electric and powered by the turning a simple crank.

Vortex manufactures such a blender, which they tout as "Great for camping trips, tailgates, or your kitchen." The cook in the campsite (or perhaps the bartender) might appreciate this development. Other features include two speeds of operation and a base that fits into the pitcher for easy, compact storage. A camper who purchased the product declared in an Internet online review: "If you're seriously gourmet, the Vortex hand crank blender is powerful enough to make soup or a sauce at your next four-course fireside meal."

Vortex Hand-Crank Blender from GSI Outdoors

TerraPass offers a hand-crank coffee grinder on its green products page. The grinding mechanism is similar to the grinder in a pepper mill. Made of stainless steel for ruggedness in the outdoors, users can adjust the mill to deliver various grades of coarseness to the ground coffee beans. Other manual grinders are available from the Internet, including a model that grinds the beans the consistency of talcum powder for bold Turkish coffee.

Hand-Cranked Rechargeables

Hand-cranking rechargeable devices are also a good choice for venturing into the wilderness. The camper or sportsman can carry along lanterns and flashlights that need no batteries or sunlight. Each comes with a hand-cranked generator that recharges an internal rechargeable battery. Some devices perform multiple functions. The Trevor Bayliss "My Mini Magic Torch, for example, is a battery-free wind-up LED torch with emergency cell phone charger. The hi-tech, brushless hand generator system will provide 25-30 minutes of light for each minute wound and is virtually immune to wear, according to product information found on the TerraPass Web site. The internal (NiMH) battery of 300mA capacity offers up to five hours of continuous light output. These torches also feature a Super Bright LED lamp tested to 50,000 hours life as well as an emergency mobile phone charger complete with Nokia auto recoil connecting wire. The unit comes with a range of adapters to suit most other popular makes.

Also available for the sportsman who wants to take some of civilization along on the trip are devices that use solar cells to operate the equipment and recharge others. There are even solar-powered rechargers for cell phones, MP3 players and other sophisticated electronics.

The Trevor Bayliss Eco Radio has three environmentally friendly sources of power: hand-crank generator, solar panel and USB charge socket. The USB socket means you can recharge the unit by plugging it into a computer. These new products are not only eco-friendly but also support multiple functions. The Eco Radio has a bright LED light for emergency use and a red LED lamp for night viewing. The radio picks up both AM and FM bands. You can use the USB port to recharge a cell phone. Trevor Bayliss made the first wind-up radio more than 16 years ago, and it has been reproduced around the world since then.

One of the most surprising things about conserving energy is in learning how much electricity is used for the most mundane activities. For example, Solio, the Universal "Hybrid" Charger, is powerful enough to charge all of your handheld electronic products at home or on the move, anywhere under the sun. The device looks similar to a three-bladed fan blade but each blade is a small solar panel. The device is called a hybrid because it can be charged with the solar cells or directly from the wall. You can then run your gadget from the internal rechargeable battery in the charger just as though you plugged it into the wall.

Using the solar panels, however, could substantially reduce the nation's carbon footprint just a few users at a time. The TerraPass web site estimates that over a 12-month period, 100,000 mobile phone users charging their phones would reduce:

- 172,500 pounds of carbon dioxide (CO_2) — equivalent in volume of 6 million basketballs.
- 412 pounds of sulphur dioxide (SO_2) — equivalent of 3.6 million ping pong balls.
- 348 pounds of oxides of nitrogen (NO_x) — equivalent of 3 million ping pong balls.

Imagine the impact to the environment if every cell phone user employed a solar charger. Or if only a million did!

Solio promotes its benefits in limiting your need to purchase and carry around multiple chargers for all of your gadgets and is your one stop charging solution for all of your products from cell phones and iPods, to digital cameras, game players, and GPS.

How to Camp Without Touching the Ground

By using a little ingenuity the environmentally conscious camper can spend the night in the woods without even leaving a print on the ground. While many think about a hammock as a device for taking a nap under a shady tree on a summer afternoon, you can also use it to create a one-person tent. Simply get in the hammock and cover it with a rain fly or mosquito netting when necessary.

The hammock tent should probably be limited to warm weather, although it is entirely possible to crawl into a sleeping bag in the hammock when temperatures get nippy. Sleeping while suspended above the ground is appealing to some people who have a fear of snakes and other night crawling creatures. Some simply are not comfortable being in contact with the cold ground.

Some hard-core backpackers like the slight curvature of a hammock after a long day of activity. The slight curvature gives a gentle stretch to tired back muscles. And by elevating the feet a bit, feet and ankles avoid the slight swelling that some experience after having hiked all day.

While the hammock is a minimalistic way to camp, tents in various materials, sizes, styles and price ranges fill the Internet sites that sell camping equipment. And just about every comfort has been reduced to battery or solar power operated. For example, you can turn tent camping in extremely hot weather into a more pleasant experience by using a tent air conditioners.

Tent Air Conditioners

KoolerAire offers 12-volt air conditioning units for cooling a tent. The user simply fills a cooler with ice and places the KoolerAire unit on the open cooler. A 12-volt van pulls in hot air, circulates it in the cooler and blows out air that has been cooled to around 50 degrees Fahrenheit, according to product information. You can even buy an adapter that allows you to use up to a 72-quart cooler or sizes in between. The power can come from your car's battery. The unit comes with an adapter to plug into a cigarette lighter.

KoolerAire Tent Air Conditioner

Earthtech Products Solar Laptop Charger and Portable Power Kit

Much more powerful air conditioners made to cool the cabin of a boat or cab of a truck are available. These run off 12-volt rechargeable batteries or even solar power. Even high-energy requirements can be met on the road or trail.

Take Any Appliance with You

RoadPro makes a line of household appliances that run on 12-volt DC power, the kind supplied by car and truck batteries. Appliances include: a soft-sided thermoelectric cooler with a capacity for 24 canned drinks; a 10-cup coffee maker; blender; fan; portable stove; ceramic heater; curling iron; air dryer; toaster oven; slow cooker; vacuum cleaner. By operating off a car battery, these appliances create no carbon footprint.

An alternative to the car battery is a 12-volt unit that can be recharged by the sun or by plugging into a regular AC outlet. There are also rechargeable units with power inverters that convert DC power from the battery into AC current as is found in the home. Some units are rechargeable via solar power. Therefore, you can get away from it all and still take it all with you without having to buy special direct current appliances. Your regular household appliances will run fine using a battery that turns battery power into an alternating current. When heading to your campsite, or even "spike" hunting, it is possible to use an electric fry pan or toaster oven straight from home.

Alternatives to Processed Fuel

One of the most energy intensive activities for a camper is cooking. Many outdoor enthusiasts use the campers' old standby, the reliable Coleman stove fueled with white gas or propane to create a fire hot enough to boil water. There are alternatives, however, to traditional fuels that allow you to take advantage of fuel sources provided by nature.

One of the least expensive and easiest-to-find fuels on a wilderness outing is sticks and twigs. These are the simple fuels that power the LittlBug cooker, a biomass-powered stove that won a design award from the Minnesota Inventor's Congress. And to my friends in Minnesota and to others who may have lived through a cold winter day on the back of a dog sled in northern Minnesota, if it passes your test, I know it must be good.

Leading my team of dogs in Ely, Minnesota

Surprisingly simple to assemble and use, the LittlBug cooker resembles a metal can cut into sections that can be easily packed and re-assembled into a cylindrical shape later at the campsite. A cooking pot is placed on the top of the cylindrical body and supported by internal curved metal pieces that fit inside the open space of the stove. An optional metal pan and chain kit enables the wilderness chef to hang the stove at a convenient and comfortable height for cooking. The metal pan can also be used on the ground to further reduce the impact of the fire to the environment. The ashes left over in the pan can be scattered after the fire has burned itself out and cooled. There should be no trace of a fire left behind.

Because twigs and small pieces of firewood found along the way are used for fuel, the camper does not have to carry in fuel or take out empty containers. In a pinch, campers can also use alcohol as a fuel. And while the fire produces smoke and carbon emissions, the firewood does not create secondary emissions the way other fuels do through chemical processing or distillation steps. A camper who follows safety rules for making and using campfires will be doing the environment a favor.

Another cooking option that does not even use an open fire and carbon producing fuel is the use of a solar oven. One kit available on the Internet provides plans for using a parabolic satellite dish as the solar energy collector. The great advantage of the kit is that an old, discarded satellite dish can be used, which significantly reduces the cost.

Other devices such as solar-powered grills use the same cooking principle, which is to position shiny panels so that they catch the suns rays and focus them on a spot that heats for cooking. Using black pots to more efficiently capture sunlight also adds to the effectiveness of solar cooking. And some cookers are designed to work similar to a greenhouse; light passes through a glass window and the heat is trapped inside to bake foods. While it takes longer for sun-powered cooking to finish, it is as effective as other methods. Temperatures can reach between 350 degrees and 450 degrees Fahrenheit.

Deluxe Sun Oven® by Sun Ovens International

While it is possible to order a pre-fabricated cooker made of a variety of materials, it's possible to find articles in books and magazines and on the Internet about making your own solar cooker. Usually cardboard, aluminum foil and a pane of glass are the only major materials required.

Some commercially available solar cooking systems, such as the Deluxe Sun Oven pictured above, even come with a thermostat to help control internal temperatures. The surprising thing about solar ovens is that they cook no matter what the outside temperature is. Ice fishermen can use them in subfreezing weather as long as the sun is shining. It is the sun's rays that are captured within the cooking area and converted to heat.

Although solar cooking uses free, carbonless energy, it does have a number of drawbacks for which adjustments must be made. Cooking should be done during the middle of the day when sunlight is strongest and most abundantly available. Also, cooking cannot be done at night or on cloudy days. Because solar cooking is slower, meals must be started earlier than normal. But since the slow cooking method requires little immediate attention, the camp cook can do other things while waiting for the main course to finish. And when cooked in heavy cookware, such as cast iron, food will stay heated for hours.

Solar ovens such as the Deluxe Sun Oven are pricey, selling for over $200. However, a wide variety are available for as little as $35. And the least cost method is "do it yourself."

The great power of the sun can be harnessed for other outdoor purposes besides cooking. A hot shower heated by the free energy of the sun is a great luxury for the wilderness camper. Some showers come with a showerhead mounted on a stand. Water capacity varies depending upon your needs and what you are willing to pay. One system allows you to connect solar tubes together to provide an 80-gallon capacity shower. This is not an item to backpack, however. Most camping showers are essentially a PVC or waterproof bag in which the water is heated after being hung in the sunshine. These cost from $15 to $20. You can also buy a freestanding tent to use as a shower shelter. Cheaper ones cost from $25 to $30. Others cost in the range of: $70 to $150. Some can serve a second function as a camping "out-house."

Getting There

American sportsmen traditionally have preferred larger vehicles that can support the weight of their equipment and caught game. Unfortunately, many older truck and SUV models tend to have lower energy efficiency and gas mileage ratings. However, technological improvements are changing our vehicles, which can help reduce our fuel costs, as well as take a step toward helping to reduce our emissions. While strides are being made in hybrid technology for vehicles, especially for heavy trucks and full-sized SUVs, the same technology can be used by us sportsmen as we hunt and fish.

When considering a new vehicle you may want to look for a model designed for better fuel and higher energy efficiency. Many people are familiar with smaller hybrids like the Toyota Prius, but larger vehicles like the Chevrolet Silverado and the Toyota Highlander 4WD now come in hybrid models. These larger hybrids are good choices for the sportsman who does not want to give up the power and versatility of an SUV but who does seek to reduce their fuel costs and emissions.

On its web site, Chevrolet announces that it is the "first manufacturer to bring you a production two-mode hybrid full-size pickup." In the first mode, at low speed and light load, the vehicle can operate in three ways: electric power, engine power or in any combination of electric and engine power. When operating with electric power, it provides all the efficiency of a full hybrid system. The second mode is used primarily at highway speeds to optimize efficiency. It provides electric assist in addition to four-cylinder or full eight-cylinder power when conditions demand it, such as trailer towing and climbing steep grades. Chevy's promotion points out the energy efficiency of the vehicle while drivers also have access to plenty of horsepower and torque.

Though the sticker price on hybrids is still generally higher than that of their non-hybrid counterparts, tax incentives, coupled with savings in gas costs over the life of the vehicle, make this choice a sound financial as well as environmental one. The 2008 Toyota Highlander, for example, was designed to give consumers an option; one version is standard gasoline-powered while the other is hybrid model. The Toyota Highlander Hybrid 4WD model costs less than $10,000 more than its gasoline-powered counterpart. Moreover, the hybrid version has 26 combined fuel economy compared to 19 combined MPG in fuel economy.[222] At about $4 per gallon of gas, the hybrid model of the Toyota Highlander can save you almost $1,000 annually compared to the standard 4WD version.

All Electric 4WD

For those sportsmen who prefer to enjoy the environment from the seat of an off-road vehicle, consider the Bad Boy Buggie or another electric All-Terrain Vehicle (ATV). Built by Bad Boy Enterprises, the Bad Boy Buggie is the first all-electric 4-wheel drive vehicle. Not only is it more environmentally friendly than traditional ATVs but hunters who have used the Bad Boy were pleasantly surprised by its stealth attributes. The quiet motor helped give these hunters an advantage over both big and small game on their hunts.[223] Barefoot Motors also offers another quiet, zero-emissions ATV that runs entirely off electricity and can be used for your recreational or agricultural activities. The company's product, Model One, is endorsed by Mythbuster's co-host, Jaime Hyneman, who hails the ATV for its environmental benefit:

> Every hour that a gas ATV is running, it's putting out as many pollutants as four modern cars because the engines don't have the same pollution restrictions. An electric ATV could be charged on the grid at a fraction of the pollution and cost associated with gas ATVs, and it would be much quieter, too.[224]

Alternative fuel vehicles are another option. These vehicles can use natural gas, hydrogen, or even propane.[225] But aside from these combined-fuel cars and trucks, vehicle developers are harvesting a more natural source for energy: the Sun. By investing in solar technology, vehicle designers and even sportsmen, like us, have found a way to reduce their emissions to nearly zero and still get around town.

People have been attempting to harness the sun's energy for power since the beginning of civilization. Solar energy has been around for millions of years. Plants, humans, and animals all naturally thrive off the energy provided by the sun, so why don't we take it a step further and use it to power our lifestyles?

Discussing solar energy in Namibia, Africa

As early as 1830, inventors like John Herschel were taking steps toward harnessing the power of the sun. Herschel found a way to cook food by using a solar energy collector.[226] This invention helped pave the way for other applications of solar-based power, such as using the Sun's abundant energy to warm homes and heat water through solar panels installed on roofs. Recently, vehicle designers have discovered new ways to collect solar energy to run land and marine vehicles. Installing solar panels and plates are an excellent way to modify your current vehicle so it runs more efficiently and is more environmentally friendly. The Solar Powered Motorcycle and ATV Battery Maintainer, for example, collect energy from the Sun and convert that energy into low-voltage electricity.[227]

In 2007, energy corporation British Petroleum (BP) commissioned Bad Boy Enterprises for their newest solar-powered ATVs. BP Solar, a division of BP, has worked on developing and utilizing cleaner technology for the last 30 years. Commercially, BP Solar is one of the largest solar energy users in the world. Moreover, solar modules designed and implemented by the company have helped to offset over 14 million metric tons of CO_2.[228] Through using BP's solar panels and modifying the electric version of the buggy, Bad Boy Enterprises became a pioneer in the solar industry, creating a quiet, non-polluting version of their already popular Bad Boy Buggy.[229]

BP liked the innovation so much that they have commissioned Bad Boy for 50 buggies to continue development in the solar industry.[230] BP has donated several of the buggies to zoos, nature preserves, universities, and wildlife departments to help park rangers and staff interact with the environment in the least intrusive way possible.[231] One more way sportsmen can move within natural habitats with limited human disruption.

As for interacting within natural water habitats, Monte Gisborne and his solar-electric Loon have caused quite a stir in the recreational boating industry. The EPA's standards encourage the use of four-stroke engines over two-stroke motors for their better efficiency. The only concern over the preferred engines, according to Gisborne, is their true environmental friendliness. No studies have yet been conducted to show the cleanliness of four-stroke engines on their own. Gisborne, who advocates alternative energy, decided to create his own pontoon boat using solar technology. His boat, The Loon, is one of a kind with a range of 30 miles using solar panels that utilize a lead-acid battery pack.[232] Over five times more efficient than a gas-powered boat, the Loon can reach speeds between five and eight knots.[233] In designing the Loon, Gisborne took many factors into consideration:

Everything from the seating arrangement to pontoon design to the propulsion system was designed to minimize man's impact on the ecosystem while maximizing enjoyment on the water.... We need sensible options if we want to leave something for future generations to enjoy.... I believe water and electricity do mix!"[234]

My fifteen foot Thresher off the Florida coast

Each and every angler among us understands and appreciates the importance of a good, quiet electric trolling motor to position our boat to enable us to hook the Big

One. The advantage of a quiet trolling motor is the absolute best practical reason to adopt electric and solar technology as a boat's main propulsion—to quietly position the boat to provide the best opportunity to cast the line and hook the fish of our dreams. We can use an electric or solar motor to rapidly get to a general area without alerting the fish to our arrival. We can use the quiet motor to our advantage to help us catch fish and at the same time we can help to preserve the environment because the old motor has been replaced with an energy efficient and environmentally friendly motor.

Solar Power for the RV and Camper

Just as solar power can be used to generate electricity for a boat, those who travel by RV or trailer can help reduce their environmental footprint by supplying some of their electricity via solar cells. The top of these vehicles provide a large area for mounting the panels. Some systems, as shown below right, allow the user to tilt the panel to achieve maximum exposure to the sun.

While many appliances such as air conditioners and heaters large enough to accommodate one of these vehicles can be converted to rechargeable batteries and solar cells, the power demand of these appliances make them impractical for total solar cell replacement. Cells can be used to power most lower voltage needs, such as computers, television, DVD players, lights and rechargers for phones and blackberry type devices.

Solar cells fit snugly on this Air Stream trailer. **Kits are available so to convert RVs to solar electricity.**

Solar Conversion Kits

Solar conversion kits are readily available on the Internet. The most expensive item is the panel of photovoltaic cells that convert sunlight to electric current. Panels can range from as little as $300 to $1,800 depending upon the amount of energy required. Other equipment includes a controller that keeps batteries fully charged and protected from overcharging. The next requirement is a battery. The batteries usually consist of one or more deep-cycle batteries that store the electric energy from the photovoltaic cells. A voltage inverter converts the direct current (DC) electricity stored in the battery to alternating current (AC), which is the type of electricity used by most household appliances.

Other necessary hardware includes connecting cables, safety devices such as circuit breakers and fuses, meters to monitor the system and other devices depending upon the complexity of the system. While the system can soon get expensive, the good news is that it is dependable, rugged and never needs mechanical repairs as does an electric generator. Also, the fuel—the sun—is free and non-polluting. So while you may be reluctant to spend the money on such new technology, you have the benefit of knowing you are little by little reducing your environmental impact in the wild.

Roofing tiles that serve as photovoltaic cells as well, left. The IllumiBrite Greenway Solar LED Pathway Lighting, center (photo courtesy of Sol Inc.), can be used in areas where there is no hook up to an electric grid. And solar charging backpacks such as the Voltaic backpack, right, allow charging of small electronic devices even on the trail.

The Solar Powered Cabin

New products developed every day make it easier for the camper/sportsman to be environmentally responsible while enjoying the great outdoors. Products such as roof shingles that are also solar cells provide a rugged covering for the roof while supplying free electricity. The manufacturer of these shingles, OkSolar, says that the system shown in the left photograph costs about $14,000 and can supply 10 to 30 percent of the energy needs for a medium-size energy efficient house. Other manufacturers of solar shingles include: Uni-Solar of Auburn Hills, Michigan; Atlantis Energy Systems with dealers all over the United States and in Europe and Canada; and Sunpower, a Silicon Valley based manufacturer.

Even if you cannot afford an entire solar electric system, a few panels can supply electricity for items such as electronic equipment and even outdoor security lights. Many manufacturers are beginning to offer street lights powered by solar. Imagine the difference it would make if the millions of streetlights throughout America were replaced with solar panels that are completely off the electric grid. The cost of electricity for security lighting for our country would be greatly reduced, resulting in great savings to taxpayers.

Solar powered rechargers are available even for the backpacker. Voltaic offers solar-charging backpacks. Charge your devices while camping, hiking, or anytime that there is sunlight. Each backpack comes with a built in solar panel, which generates four watts of solar power for quick charging of handheld electronics. Also, a battery pack is included which stores excess solar power for whenever you need it, even on a cloudy day. Just expose the solar panel to sunlight.

Solar Water Heating for a Cabin

Because the average home uses 30 percent of its total energy just to heat water, a solar water heating system can mean great savings. Most systems circulate water through tubes exposed to sunlight. In some systems the circulation is passive, created by the physics principle that hot liquids rise and cold liquids fall. Other systems use electric pumps to circulate the water. This means electricity is needed in most cases.

Naturally, the sun is not always available, so it is generally difficult for a homeowner to get 100 percent of the hot water needed for the household. Nevertheless, it is reasonable to assume a solar system could provide 50 to 80 percent of needed hot water.

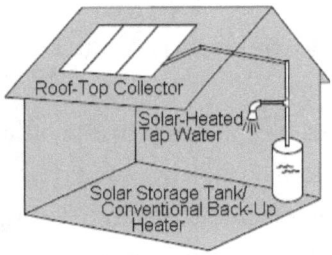

A typical solar water heater consists of a collector that collects the heat from the sun, usually via a circulating liquid, a system for using the heated liquid to heat cold tap water in a tank and a distribution system for the hot water.

For a cabin in a remote area of the woods, solar heating hot water would be an effective way to enjoy the civilized luxury of a hot shower. If a passive solar system were used, then no electricity would be required at all. However, a photovoltaic panel on the roof could supply the small amount of power needed for a water pump.

While a commercially installed solar water heating system can cost three or four times a conventional water heater, it lasts 15 to 40 years. The best part is that the hot water created is free. The sportsman may find it useful to test a solar water heating system at his getaway and install a similar system at home where constant use would make the savings far greater.

For the modern equipped home-away-from-home, solar water heaters are available for real energy hogs such as a hot tub or Jacuzzi and heated swimming pool.

Recycle to Help Nature

While recycling helps to conserve natural resources, promotes energy efficiency and assists in protecting the environment, it also benefits our mutual interests in another way—recycling allows game to successfully thrive in its natural habitat. Without recycling, landfills would quickly reach capacity. This means more space would be needed to either expand an existing landfill or create a completely new one. In any event, the land taken to serve as additional landfill space is land that would otherwise be used as a natural habitat for wildlife. By recycling, we can extend the life of existing landfills and delay—and in some instances even prevent—infringing upon natural habitats to store our waste. Recycling ensures we do not unnecessarily take away land that belongs to our game.

This also ensures we as sportsmen will continue to have game to hunt and fish.

Few in this country care about the environment and its natural inhabitants as much we sportsmen do. We know first-hand the importance of a pristine, natural environment to the wildlife that inhabits these areas. Without the natural environment, wildlife will cease to exist as we know it, and our ability and appreciation for enjoying the environment as sportsmen will also cease to exist. No land means no wildlife. No wildlife means no hunting or fishing. It's that simple. We have a responsibility to conserve our undeveloped lands and wildlife, and the easiest and most effective way we can do so is for each of us to recycle.

Environmentally Responsible Hunting Gear and Supplies

Some companies that cater to the outdoorsman are now becoming more conscious of their own environmental impact when manufacturing and designing outdoor gear.

One major cause for concern is the amount of lead used in the manufacturing of some hunting and fishing equipment. In recent years, scientists have concluded that even ingesting a small amount of lead can be dangerous to wildlife. The U.S. Geological Survey reports that lead from bullets and sinkers has been found in the mouths and digestive systems of reptiles, waterfowl, birds of prey and even small mammals. It is even possible that lead contaminants can damage hunting and fishing grounds, further harming our plant and wildlife.[235]

Promoting the use of alternative sporting equipment also can be a great way to reduce your environmental impact and save money. Try looking for products that are tested for environmental safety and are non-toxic. It is possible that by purchasing some newer, more efficient items for your home, your job or your trip can make a large difference.

Standing Up for the American Sportsman

Governments and politicians can go back and forth on just what the causes of global climate change are and what the nations of the world can and should do about it. The American sportsman has a different agenda and a different constituency to answer to—themselves. Since America's founding, this nation's outdoorsmen have had a unique understanding of the relationship between man and nature and just what needs to be done to maintain that delicate balance. It is up to us, again, to accept our position as a force to be reckoned with in defending and protecting our environment. We who make our livings or enjoy our recreation in the great outdoors can take positive steps toward limiting our environmental footprint by making and remaining committed to small changes in the way we interact with the environment. We cannot count on the politicians and environmental groups to take our interests into account if we haven t taken a seat at the table. It is time for the American sportsmen and sportswomen to restore our rightful place among environmentalists and conservationists to ensure the preservation of our way of life for future generations.

222 <http://www.toyota.com/compare/index.html#h_overview>.
223 "Bad Boy Buggies: All Electric 4WD." *Bad Boy Buggies Hill Country.* <http://www.badboybuggieshillcountry.com/>.
224 Hyneman, Jaime. Qtd in "Barefoot Motors Testimonials." May 2008. *Popular Mechanic.* <http://barefootmotors.com/testimonials01.php?display=hyneman&view=hynemanvideo>.
225 "Alternative Fuels." *U.S. Department of Energy.* <http://www.fueleconomy.gov/feg/current.shtml>.
226 Alliant Energy. "Solar Power." *Alliant Energy Kids.* <http://www.alliantenergykids.com/stellent2/groups/public/documents/pub/phk_ee_re_001505.hcsp>.
227 "Solar Powered Motorcycle and ATV Battery Maintainer." 2008. *Batteries.com.* <http://www.batteries.com/productprofile.asp?appid=230307>.
228 <http://www.bp.com/sectiongenericarticle.do?categoryId=8051&contentId=7036665>.
229 "BP Donates Solar Utility Vehicle to Audubon Zoo During Earth Fest." Press Release. *Bad Boy Buggies.* 26 March 2007. <http://www.badboybuggies.com/news.htm>.
230 Hall, Natalie. "Execs Test-Drive Solar Powered Vehicle." *Bad Boy Buggies.* 29 May 2007. <http://www.badboybuggies.com/news.htm>.
231 "BP Donates Bad Boy Buggy to Lakeshore Nature Preserve." *Bad Boy Buggies.* <http://www.badboybuggies.com/news.htm>.
232 Carter, Lauren. "S.O.S.: Polluting Boat Ahead." May-June 2007. *E: The Environmental Magazine.* <http://findarticles.com/p/articles/mi_m1594/is_3_18/ai_n27280474>.
233 "Monte Gisborne's Solar Loon." *Solar Navigator.* 2006. <http://www.solarnavigator.net/solar_loon.htm>.
234 *Ibid.*
235 "Lead from Hunting and Fishing Build Millions of Pounds of Pollutants Annually." *California Green Solutions.* 13 July 2008. <http://www.californiagreensolutions.com/cgi-bin/gt/tpl.h,content=2396>.

ABOUT THE AUTHOR

As a senior environmental attorney with the Charlotte law firm of Moore & Van Allen, Tom Mullikin leads the firm's Government, Policy and Regulatory Affairs Team. His practice focuses on corporate compliance, regulatory relations and legislative representation. Tom's career spans more than twenty years and includes key legislative staff roles, direct legislative advocacy, extensive environmental legal representation and management of environmental and energy issue campaigns for industry.

Tom works with clients to address the practical social, political, and environmental impacts of climate change. He has been recognized as a Distinguished Lecturer on climate change at the Illinois' Governors State University and at Loyola University New Orleans, and presented in the University of the Ozarks Distinguished Speaker Series. He has spoken on the intersection of the economy and our environmental challenges at international conferences in Australia, Russia, and the Czech Republic, and across the United States in conjunction with industry associations and state and regional chambers of commerce.

In 2005, Tom led a team of researchers and environmental experts on an Antarctica expedition studying the effects of climate change on the polar regions. He told the story of this expedition in a video documentary, *Climate Change: Global Problems, Global Solutions*, which received widespread acclaim in both business and environmental circles, and was broadcast on New Hampshire Public Television, with a Boston-area viewership of more than 2.4 million households. He has led subsequent expeditions to the Namib Desert of Africa, the Amazon River Basin of Peru, and the Great Barrier Reef of Australia to highlight the global effects of climate change.

Tom is the author of *The Maxims of Politics: Making Government Work*, *Global Solutions: Demanding Total Accountability for Climate Change*, and *Truck Stop Politics: Understanding the Emerging Force of Working Class America*. He has been widely published in both legal and mainstream periodicals, including *UCLA Journal of Environmental Law and Policy*, *Georgetown International Environmental Law Review*, *Campaigns and Elections Magazine*, *South Carolina Jurisprudence*, *Navigating the Government Contracts Process*, and *Vital Speeches of the Day*. Further, he has been quoted for his experience in both the law and the environment by *Los Angeles Times*, *Newsday*, *Associated Press*, *St. Petersburg (Fla.) Times*, *Charlotte Observer*, *Richmond Times Dispatch*, *Roanoke-Chowan News-Herald*, *Duluth News Tribune*, *Hibbing Daily Tribune*, *Wichita Eagle*, *Business North*, *Business News Publishing Co.*, *Rocky Mountain News*, *Salt Lake Tribune*, *Post and Courier*, *Hamilton Spectator*, *Natural Awakenings Charlotte*, and *Huntinamibia*.

Tom previously served as Chief Counsel and Vice President for Public Affairs to the largest environmental services company in the world. He has served on state legislative and congressional staff, and as an advisor and campaign manager to senior members of Congress and U.S. Presidential candidates from both the Republican and Democratic parties.

Tom formerly served with the United States Army Judge Advocate General Corps, USAR, where he served as the Assistant Staff Judge Advocate for the 360th Civil Affairs Brigade (Airborne), United States Army Civil Affairs and Psychological Operations, United States Army Special Operations Command. For his service, he was awarded, among other honors, the Meritorious Service Medal, Army Achievement Medal, and Global War on Terror Service Medal. He has also received the Order of the Palmetto, the highest civilian honor bestowed by the State of South Carolina.

www.mvalaw.com
www.sportsmanenvironmentalist.com

www.ingramcontent.com/pod-product-compliance
Lightning Source LLC
LaVergne TN
LVHW091553060526
838200LV00036B/823